Basic
SOAP MAKING

All the Skills and Tools You Need to Get Started

Elizabeth Letcavage, editor

Patsy Buck,
soap maker and
expert consultant

Photographs by
Alan Wycheck

STACKPOLE
BOOKS

Copyright © 2009 by Stackpole Books

Published by
STACKPOLE BOOKS
5067 Ritter Road
Mechanicsburg, PA 17055
www.stackpolebooks.com

Printed in China

10 9 8 7 6 5 4 3 2 1

First edition

Cover design by Tracy Patterson

Library of Congress Cataloging-in-Publication Data

Basic soap making: all the skills and tools you need to get started / Elizabeth Letcavage, editor ; Patsy Buck, soap maker and expert consultant ; photographs by Alan Wycheck. — 1st ed.
    p. cm.
  ISBN-13: 978-0-8117-3573-5
  ISBN-10: 0-8117-3573-7
1. Soap. I. Letcavage, Elizabeth. II. Buck, Patsy.

TP991.B365 2009
668'.12—dc22
                               2008050851

Contents

Foreword

Making your own soap is both an intriguing and rewarding experience. It's intriguing in that you can see the ingredients turn from a thin clear or amber liquid to a thick opaque mixture right before your eyes. The rewards come after your soap cures and you're able to reap the benefits and the luxury of using a product you made.

I started making soap because I was having adverse reactions to many of the so-called "hypoallergenic" soaps on the market. I started purchasing handmade soap at craft fairs and other places. Although these were all nice soaps, they seemed to be a bit wrong for me: wrong fragrance, too scratchy from additives, too drying. The more I read about soap making, the more I became convinced that I could make soap that suited my skin type.

Since then, I have made many successful batches and quite a few that won't be made again. Today, there are online soap calculators that can make the job of determining the lye-to-oil ratio much easier than when I first sat with paper, pencil, a table of SAP values, and a handheld calculator to figure out my first soap recipes.

This book will provide you with a photo-by-photo account of the soap-making process and a sampling of basic recipes to get you started. When you progress to creating your own recipes, keep a notebook (with pictures if you like) of all the ingredients and additives you use and changes you make. I hope you enjoy making cold process soap as much as I do and that this book helps you make wonderful soap for you, your family, and your friends.

Happy soap making.

—Patsy Buck

Introduction

A bar of cold process soap isn't fancy. It has an old-fashioned look, similar to something the American colonists or pioneers would have used. And indeed, they did.

The procedures for making this type of soap haven't changed much over the centuries. The process starts with a lye and water solution that is added to a combination of liquid oils, solid oils, fats, and/or butters. Some of the liquid oils used include canola, corn, olive, peanut, and safflower. Solid oils are coconut and palm. Fats are lard and tallow. Butter options include cocoa and shea.

Each oil contributes different properties to the soap. For example, coconut oil creates a hard bar with a hearty lather. Olive oil makes for a stable lather and a soap that conditions the skin. Cocoa butter makes a firm conditioning bar with a stable lather. The charts in the soap recipes chapter show the beneficial properties of the various oils and butters.

Oils become soap when combined with lye and water through a process called saponification. Lye is the chemical sodium hydroxide (NaOH). Great care is essential when handling lye, a caustic alkali that can burn skin and cause blindness. Please read the safe-handling information on page 8 before starting your soap-making project.

When lye is added to water, it becomes very hot. The solution is allowed to cool and then added to the oils. This mixture is stirred until it thickens but can still be poured out of the container. This is called stirring until "trace."

Knowing the point at which trace is reached is perhaps the trickiest part of soap making and is learned through practice. Understirring the soap mixture may result in liquid pockets of lye in the bar. Overstirring causes the mixture to become very thick and unpourable.

The recipes in this book will yield lightly scented, natural-colored bars that cleanse the skin well yet are gentle enough for your hands, face, and body. Although not necessary to achieve a fine finished product, added scents, colors, and botanicals can spice up your bars. Chapter 3 on soap additives will guide you through this process.

With or without additives, you will pour the soap into a mold. To enable the "raw" soap to cure, you will put it to "bed" by covering the mold with wood or cardboard and wrapping it in towels or old blankets.

After twenty-four hours, the soap can be safely handled. It is then removed from the mold and cut into bars. The bars are placed in open air for about a month to dry and cure.

Before commercial soap manufacturers started mass-producing soap, handmade cold process soap was a necessity. Today, it's a luxury. You can make your soap without the chemical additives of store-bought soap. You can make it to suit your skin type and cleansing needs. You can select from an array of colors and fragrances or choose to add none at all.

Handmade soap also serves as an unusual yet practical gift that friends and family will appreciate. Chapter 4 illustrates how to rebatch your soap into fun, fancy shapes. Chapter 6 offers ideas for packaging your soap for gift giving.

Once a necessary household chore, making soap at home has been transformed into a relaxing craft that involves many creative options. Enjoy!

1

Basic Equipment and Ingredients

Chances are that you have most of the equipment you need to make soap right around the house. The equipment and ingredients you don't have are easily found in grocery stores or online. As you gain experience making cold process soap, you might want to make your own wooden mold, mold liner, and soap cutter. Instructions for doing so are included in chapter 7. In the meantime, easy-to-find alternatives will work almost as well.

Equipment

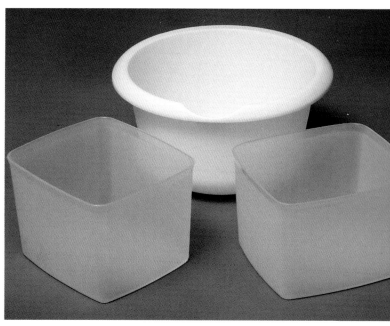

PLASTIC OR GLASS CONTAINERS
A variety of 1-quart freezer-weight plastic or 2-cup heat-safe glass measuring cups work well to measure and hold soap-making ingredients until they are mixed. *Aluminum containers are not to be used, as they will react with the lye.*

PLASTIC OR GLASS BOWLS
Use a 1½-quart heavy-weight plastic mixing bowl or a 4-quart heat-safe glass measuring cup with a handle to make one batch of soap.

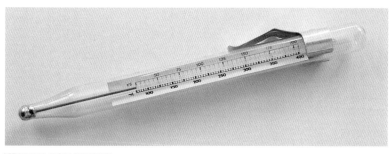

THERMOMETER
To precisely measure the temperature of the lye and water solution, you will need a thermometer. A candy-making thermometer is not costly and is available at kitchen shops, grocery stores, and craft stores. For safety's sake, it's best to dedicate this tool to soap making.

COFFEE GRINDER OR MORTAR AND PESTLE
The fast way to prepare soap additives such as oatmeal is to use an electric coffee grinder. A mortar and pestle work just as well to grind dry ingredients—it just takes a little longer to do it by hand.

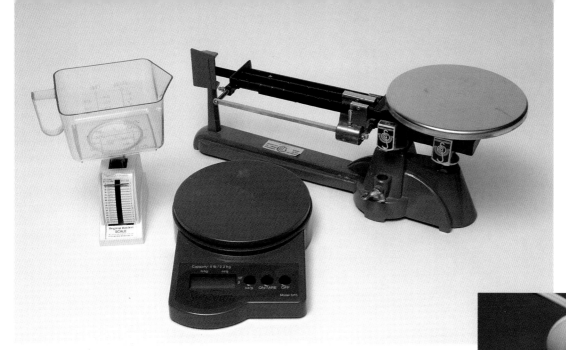

SCALE

Almost all soap-making ingredient measurements are by weight, not volume. To make a single batch of soap, a small spring scale will suffice for measuring out ingredients. For larger batches, you might want to purchase a counterbalance or electronic scale that can measure heavier weights. Scales are found in kitchen shops or in the kitchen sections of department and discount stores.

IMMERSION BLENDER (OPTIONAL)

Also called a stick blender, this tool will substantially speed up the process of mixing ingredients. Many experienced soap makers use immersion blenders instead of hand stirrers. Be careful to use only immersion blenders that do not have aluminum shafts or blades—check the packaging to determine if yours does.

SOAP MOLDS

Any nonaluminum container that will produce a rectangular log can be used. The basic soap recipes in this book are calculated to fill a 3½-inch wide, 6-inch long, 2½-inch deep mold. Suitably sized plastic food containers or cardboard boxes lined with freezer-weight plastic bags work well, too. (Instructions for making a wooden mold and mold liner are offered in chapter 7.)

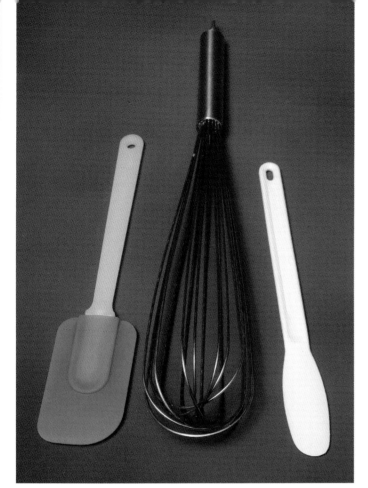

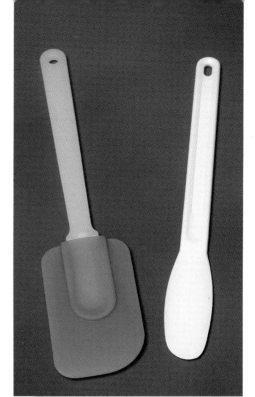

STIRRER FOR LYE

Use only utensils made from rubber, silicon, or stainless steel. *Do not use aluminum utensils, as they will react with lye, or wooden utensils, which will splinter and disintegrate when in contact with lye.*

STIRRER FOR SOAP

If you choose to stir the soap mixture by hand, select the tool with which you are most comfortable, as the process can be lengthy. Choose plastic, silicon, or rubber spatulas and spoons or a stainless steel wire whisk. *Do not use aluminum or wooden utensils.*

VEGETABLE PEELER

A common kitchen vegetable peeler is used in the finishing process to take uneven edges off the soap bars.

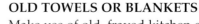

OLD TOWELS OR BLANKETS

Make use of old, frayed kitchen or bath towels and blankets. They are used to keep soap warm after it is poured into the mold. Clean towels or rags should also be kept close at hand to mop up spills or splashes.

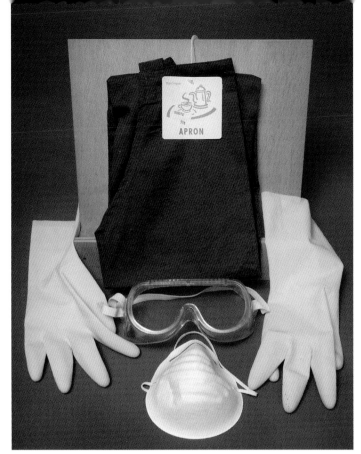

DRYING SURFACE

When placed underneath stacks of soap, plastic needlework canvas allows air circulation to dry the soap adequately before it is used. Plastic-coated window screen also works.

SAFETY GEAR

Kitchen dishwashing gloves
Three-sided protective goggles
Full-length apron to protect chest and legs
Long-sleeved shirt
Closed-toed shoes (no sandals)
Face mask (needed when working with lye)

PLASTIC STORAGE CONTAINERS

Dollar stores and craft stores are good sources for inexpensive plastic storage containers. Cardboard boxes may also be used. Soap is stored in the open air, so no lid is required.

BOARD SCRAPER/CHOPPER

You'll need a board scraper/chopper with a 6-inch blade to cut soaps made with the basic recipes. These are available at department stores and kitchen shops. (Instructions for making your own soap cutter appear in chapter 7.)

Ingredients

Most of the ingredients needed to make soap are available at the grocery store. Sources for purchasing specialty items, such as botanic additives and fragrances, are listed in the resources chapter.

LIQUID OILS

Shown here are just some of the liquid oils that may be used to make cold process soap. Most are available in grocery stores or warehouse club stores. Charts on pages 99 and 100 show the soap-making properties of the most popular oils. It's important to select 100 percent pure oils, rather than less expensive blended oils, which are a combination of two or more oils. Oils have a shelf life, so check the expiration date before using them. Spoiled or rancid oil has a foul odor and should be discarded.

SOLID OILS

Solid oils are melted in the microwave or on the stovetop before they are combined with liquid oils. (The cooking shortening Crisco® is a blend of soybean and cottonseed oils and can be used for soap making.)

BUTTERS

Avocado, shea, and cocoa butters are melted before they are mixed with liquid oils. They make soap milder and act as emollients to moisturize skin. Health food stores and pharmacies are good sources for these butters.

DISTILLED WATER

Always use distilled water for soap making instead of tap water, which may contain unwanted chlorine and minerals. Grocery and discount stores sell distilled water.

Safe Handling of Lye

Lye is a dangerous chemical that requires great care when handling. It can cause chemical burns, scarring, or permanent injury if it comes in contact with skin and blindness if it gets in the eyes. Lye may be fatal if swallowed.

When combined with water to make soap, lye becomes extremely hot, and the resulting heat may cause burns or ignite flammables.

Also, mixing lye with water to make soap causes a chemical reaction that creates fumes. Always mix lye in a well-ventilated area, and wear a face mask when mixing.

In addition, lye should not come in contact with anything made of aluminum. It will combine to produce hydrogen gas, which is explosive. Lye also reacts with various sugars to produce carbon monoxide, which is a poisonous gas.

Lastly, if exposed to air, lye will dissolve or "melt." Always keep lye in an airtight, nonmetallic container.

Always follow these safe lye-handling practices:

- Keep lye away from skin, eyes, mouth, and clothing.
- Do not handle lye in the presence of children or animals.
- Keep lye in a dry, sealed, nonmetallic container.
- Keep lye in a locked or secure area so that children or animals cannot access it.
- Keep lye away from aluminum and sugars.
- Always mix lye and water in a well-ventilated area.
- Always wear protective clothing when handling lye.

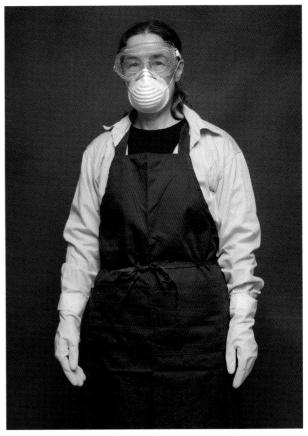

Always wear protective clothing when handling lye and raw soap.

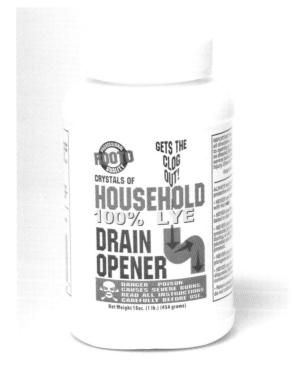

LYE

Lye comes in crystal form. Always use a product that is labeled "100 percent lye" or called "caustic soda" or "sodium hydroxide." Rooto is the brand most often found in hardware stores. See the resources page for vendors that sell lye.

8

2

Making Cold Process Soap

Begin by assembling all your ingredients and reviewing the instructions on handling lye safely. Once you've mastered this recipe, use the same procedure to make the other soap recipes that appear in the book. Then use your imagination to make your own unique blends by combining various liquid and solid oils, essential oil scents, colors, and botanic additives.

Basic Four-Oil Soap Recipe

4 ounces solid coconut oil (112 grams)
3 ounces canola oil (84 grams)
4 ounces olive oil (112 grams)
4 ounces safflower oil (112 grams)
2 ounces lye (56 grams)
5 ounces distilled water (140 grams)

Note: All measurements are by weight, not volume.

9

1. The first step in soap making is to put on protective goggles, face mask, gloves, and apron. Wear a long-sleeved shirt, long pants, and closed-toed shoes. Make sure the room in which you're working is well ventilated.

2. Place a 1-quart container on the scale and "tare" the scale. To tare an electronic scale, adjust the setting so it registers 0 after you put the container on it. This way, when you fill the container, you can measure only the ingredient, not the container, too. To tare a spring scale, adjust the position of the indicator so that it coincides with 0 on the scale. If you are using a counterbalance scale, adjust the counterweights so that the scale registers 0.

3. Slowly pour distilled water into the container. The water should be at room temperature. Add water until the scale reads 5 ounces. Remove the container from the scale and set it aside.

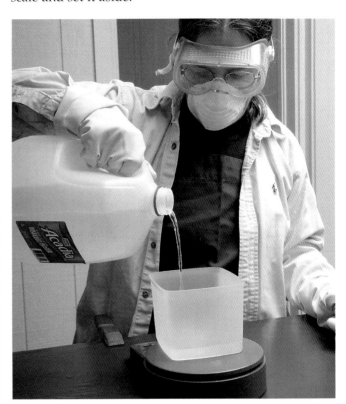

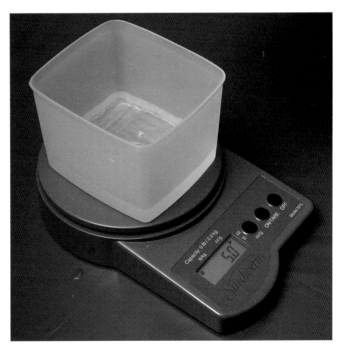

4. Place a clean, dry, empty 1-quart container on the scale and tare the scale. Then slowly begin pouring the lye into the container.

5. Continue pouring slowly until the scale indicates that you have exactly 2 ounces of lye. Precise measurements are necessary. If you poured out too much, pour some of the lye back into the original container and try again.

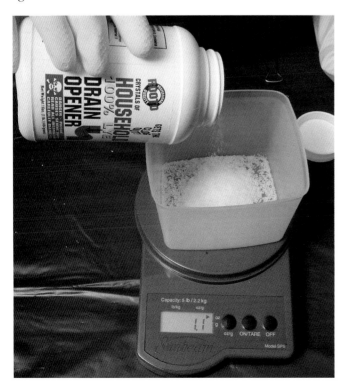

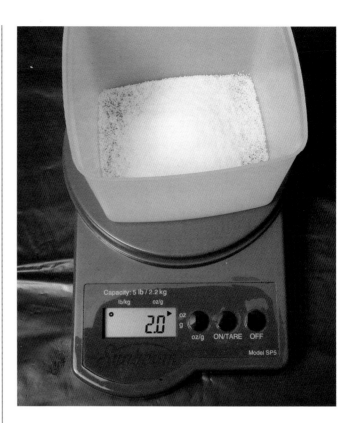

6. Slowly and carefully pour the lye into the container of distilled water. *Never pour water into the lye.* Make sure you don't splash. A chemical reaction will start taking place immediately, and the solution will become hot. It is normal to see steam coming out of the container and smell a foul odor.

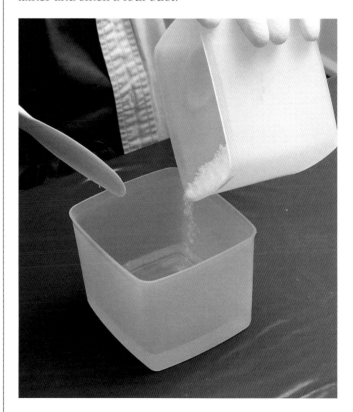

7. Immediately begin stirring the lye and water mixture gently with a plastic or silicon spoon. Stir until you can no longer see any lye crystals. (The more lye that is used in the solution, the longer it will take for the lye to dissolve.)

8. Set the lye solution aside to cool; it will be ready to mix with oils when it is clear and a thermometer shows a temperature reading of about 100 degrees F. (Experienced soap makers learn to gauge temperature by placing their hands on the outside of the container, and when the container temperature feels to be the same temperature as their hands, they know the solution is ready to be mixed with the oils.)

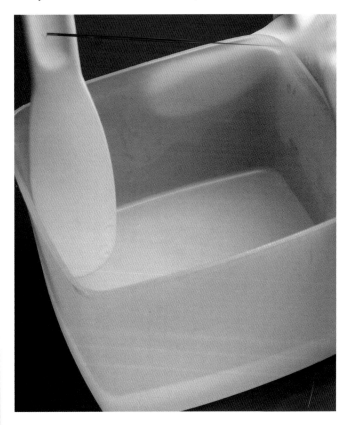

Preparing the Oils

While the lye and water solution cools, you will need to prepare the various oils that will be added to the mixture. You will first prepare the coconut oil.

1. Place a 1-quart container on the scale and tare the scale. Scoop out solid coconut oil with a spoon or spatula and place it in the container.

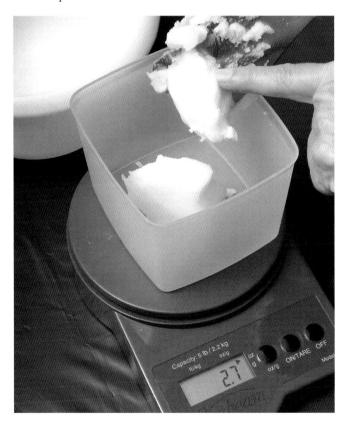

2. Continue adding the coconut oil until you have 4 ounces.

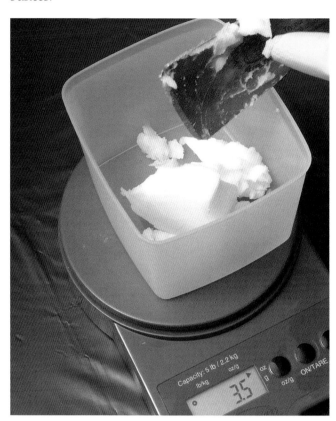

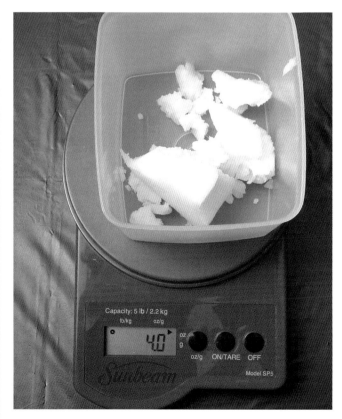

3. Use a spatula to scoop out the measured coconut oil into a 1½-quart plastic or microwave-safe bowl.

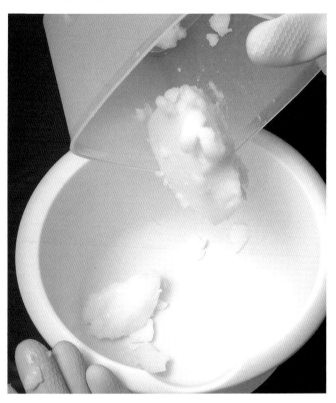

4. Place the bowl containing the oil in the microwave and microwave for 20 seconds on high power.

5. Take it out of the oven and stir. If the coconut oil has not melted, return it to the microwave and heat it again for 20 seconds. Repeat the process until all the solid coconut oil has liquefied. Remember that microwaves vary in wattage, so you may need to adjust the time or power setting to achieve the desired results.

The melted coconut oil is ready to be combined with the other oils.

Safety Note: Never leave the microwave unattended while you are heating oil. It can catch fire quickly if heated for too long at a high temperature.

6. The next step is to prepare the olive oil. Place a 1-quart plastic container on the scale and tare the scale.

7. Carefully pour 4 ounces of olive oil into the container.

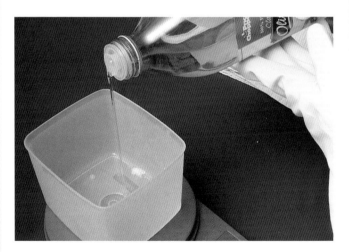

8. Again, precise measurements are necessary—if you poured out too much, pour the excess back into the bottle and try again.

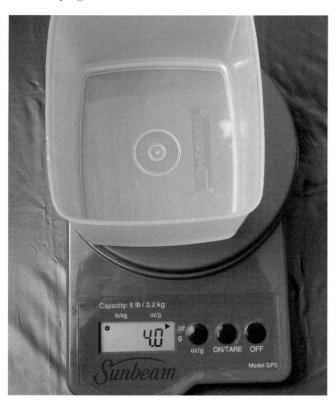

9. The canola oil is next. Repeat the process by placing a 1-quart plastic container on the scale and then taring the scale.

10. Carefully pour canola oil into the container until you have exactly 3 ounces.

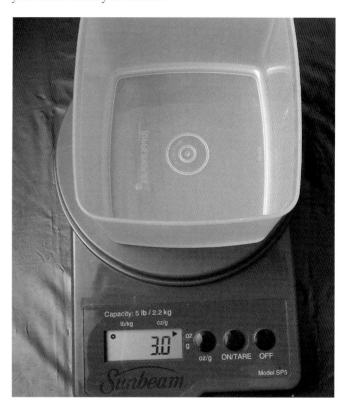

11. Repeat the process once again for the safflower oil. Place a 1-quart plastic container on the scale, then tare the scale.

12. Carefully pour out 4 ounces of safflower oil into the container.

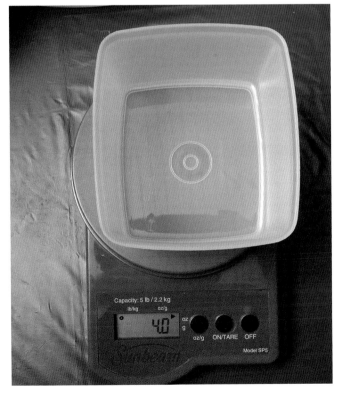

Combining the Ingredients

Once you have prepared all your oils, you are ready to mix all of the ingredients together.

1. Start by adding the olive oil to the 1½-quart container holding the melted coconut oil.

2. Use a spatula to scrape as much olive oil out of the 1-quart container as possible, then set the emptied container aside.

3. Repeat the process by pouring the container of canola oil into the 1½-quart container that now holds the coconut and olive oils.

4. Use a spatula to scrape as much of the canola oil out of the container as you can, then set the empty container aside.

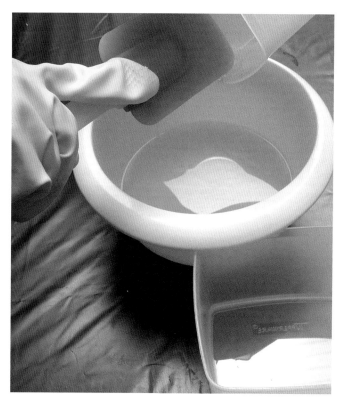

5. Repeat the same process by pouring the container of safflower oil into the container that now holds the other oils.

6. Make sure you get all of the safflower oil.

7. Gently stir until all four oils are thoroughly combined.

This lye and water solution is clear, has cooled to about 100 degrees F, and is ready to be added to the oil mixture.

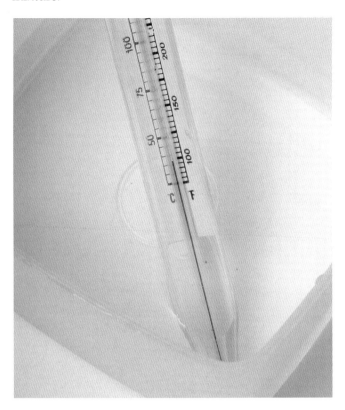

8. Being careful not to splash, slowly pour the lye and water solution into the 1½-quart container that holds the four blended oils. The lye and water mixture is heavier than the oils and will sink to the bottom.

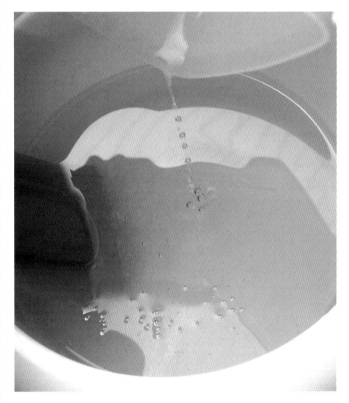

20

9. Use a spatula to gently stir the lye and oil mixture.

10. The mixture will become slightly opaque (rather than clear) as you stir. When it does, you can either continue stirring by hand or switch to the immersion blender.

11. If you use an immersion blender, submerge the blender blades into the mixture first, then turn on the blender to the low setting. As you mix, keep the blades under the surface of the mixture to prevent any from being splashed out of the container.

12. Use the immersion blender in bursts of not more than 20 or 30 seconds. After stirring for several minutes, the mixture will become thicker and more opaque. The time it takes for the soap mixture to reach trace will largely depend on the temperature of the mixture, so it will vary from batch to batch. If you stir by hand, the process could easily take about twice as long as with the immersion blender.

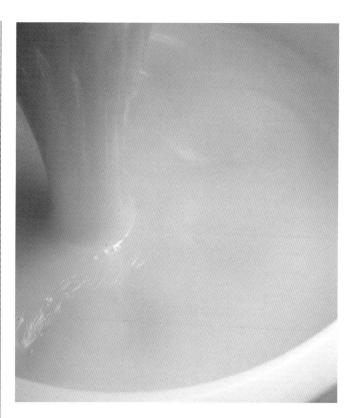

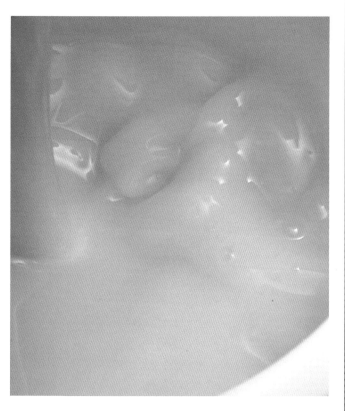

13. Start checking the mixture to see if it easily runs off your blender or spatula. As the solution thickens, it will drip off more slowly.

22

14. Once the mixture starts resembling the consistency of a pudding mixture (before it has set), the batch is close to being ready to mold. If you are using a blender, switch to a spatula and continue stirring.

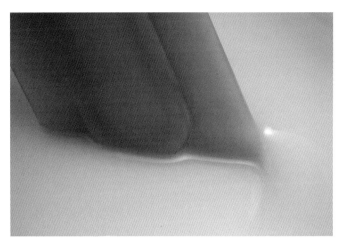

15. The key to determining when trace is reached is the spatula test. Pull the spatula out of the mixture every 10 seconds or so to check the flow of liquid. At this point, it should be dripping off the spatula more and more slowly.

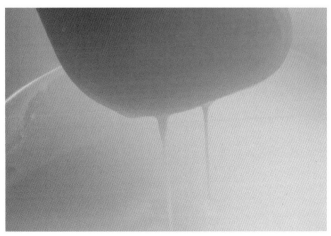

16. The point called "trace" is reached when the soap mixture that falls from your spatula leaves a trail of soap on the surface of the mixture for a few seconds before it disappears. When the mixture reaches trace, stop stirring.

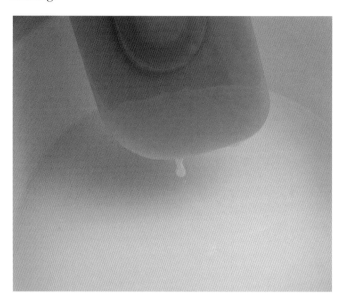

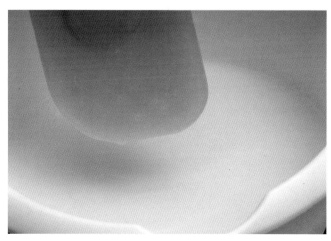

The time it takes to reach trace will be different for every recipe you use. It is at this point that you would incorporate any additives such as fragrance, color, or botanicals. Refer to chapter 3 for step-by-step instructions on incorporating these ingredients.

17. The next step is to pour the mixture into a mold. Instructions for making a wooden mold and liner are included in chapter 7. You can also use a heavy plastic food container that is about 3½ inches long, 6 inches wide, and 2½ inches deep.

18. Slowly pour the thickened soap mixture into your mold to avoid splashing and to keep air bubbles from forming in the mixture.

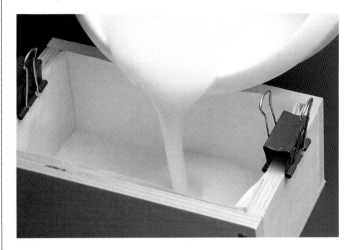

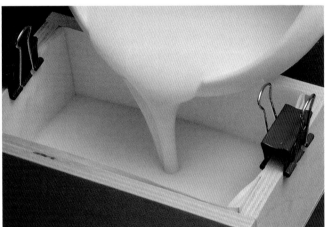

19. Use a spatula to scrape the bowl clean.

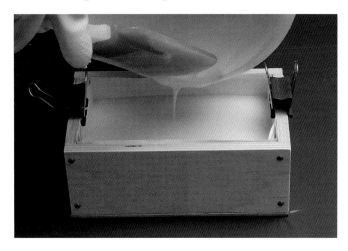

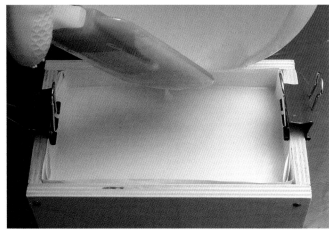

This is what your filled mold should look like. If the mixture did not flow easily into the mold, or if you have bumps on the surface, you probably overstirred the mix. Some imperfections such as these can be eliminated when you cut your soap into bars, which is covered later in the book.

Putting the Soap to Bed

The next step is to put the soap to "bed" so it can heat up and fully saponify.

1. Remove the binder clips from the mold box.

2. Place the lid over the box, making sure it is on straight and completely covering the mold.

3. Move the box to a warm location where it will remain undisturbed for at least 24 hours and be out of reach of children and pets.

4. Drape an old towel or blanket over the box to insulate the soap. This allows the soap to heat up and complete the saponification process.

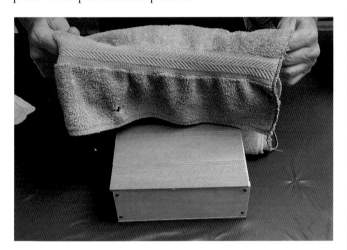

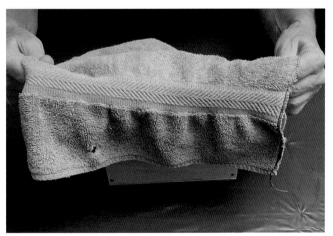

5. Tuck in all four sides of the towel, but do not put any of the towel under the box as it must remain level.

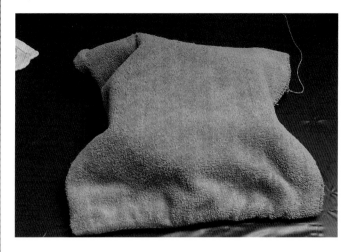

6. Drape a second towel or blanket over the first and gently tuck in the sides. Do not disturb the covered mold for 24 hours.

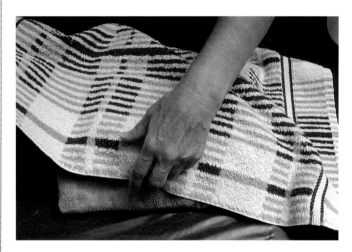

Keeping soap warm is essential to making a good batch. Here, the darker portion of the soap has reached the gel stage of the saponification process. The lighter-colored outer rim has yet to reach gel stage.

This soap did not get hot enough to properly saponify. The result is a crumbly soap with uneven color and a rough texture. This happens when the lye and water solution cools below the 100-degree recommended temperature or if the oils are cooler than room temperature when used.

Yellow, orange, or brown spots indicate that the oils in the soap are reacting with the air and are turning rancid. Finished cold process soap should last about two years, but when these spots appear, the soap should be discarded or used promptly.

You must wait at least 24 hours to clean the bowls, utensils, and blender you used to make cold process soap. Until the chemical reaction is complete, the lye in the soap mixture will remain caustic. After 24 hours, however, the residue of the soap mixture will be safe to handle. For safety's sake, it's recommended that you place your bowl and utensils in a protected place where they may not be accessed by children or pets for 24 hours.

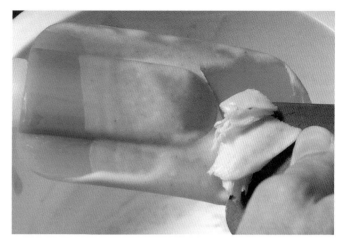

Clean up your equipment the day after you make your soap. Use a scraper or other nonmetallic or nonwooden utensil to remove soap from the spatula. Try to remove as much residue from your utensils as you can. You can put the soap residue you remove into a plastic container with no lid or into a slow cooker for reuse. Or you may discard the remaining soap by rolling it up in several layers of newspaper and placing it in the trash.

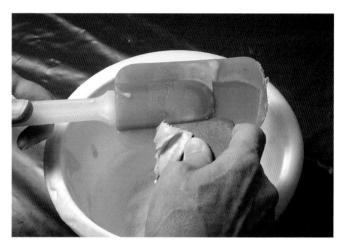

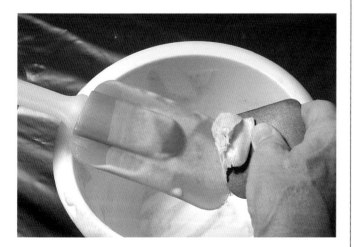

Cleanup is a treat for your hands. At this stage, the soap residue has not hardened but is safe to handle. Use your fingers to clean off your utensils. Rinse thoroughly and dry.

Of course, you will want to make sure your immersion blender is unplugged when you clean it. The best tools to use to remove the soap are your fingers. Save water by using your bowl to swish the blender as you remove the soap residue. Rinse and dry the blender thoroughly. Finish by cleaning and rinsing the bowl.

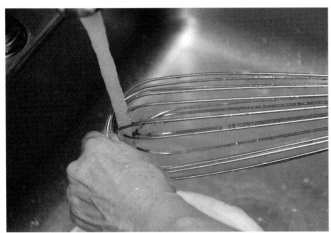

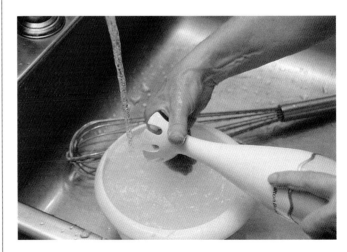

After 24 hours have passed since you poured your soap into its mold, it is safe to handle. You can then begin the process of unmolding and cutting the soap.

1. Remove the towels and the lid from the box. Hold the box by its bottom with one hand and cover the top with the other hand. Turn the box upside down and gently shake until the mold and liner are released.

2. Place the box on its side. Grasp the short ends of the mold liner and pull the soap log from the mold. The procedure is the same if you are using a lined cardboard box. If you are using a plastic container without a mold liner, however, you may need to pull the sides of the container away from the soap log to release it from the mold.

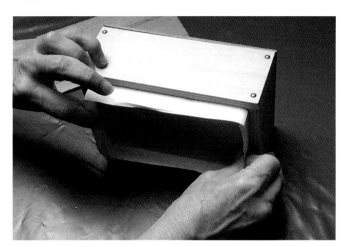

3. Place the soap log flat on the table. Remove the mold liner slowly by pulling it off the four sides with a steady, even pull. Remember, at this point, the soap is still soft.

4. Once all four sides are removed from the soap log, tip the log on its long side and peel away the remaining mold paper. If the mold liner is not torn, you can reuse it to make another batch of soap.

5. Although the soap is safe to handle after 24 hours, it's a good practice to use your rubber gloves when cutting the newly cured soap log into bars. To do so, place the soap log on a piece of plastic canvas or cutting board to protect the table from being damaged by the knife blade. Set the blade of the scraper/chopper 1 inch from the end of the log and at a 90-degree angle from the soap surface. You may make your bars any width, but a 1-inch bar is a good size. With both hands, use firm and even pressure to push the blade downward until you cut all the way through the log. Keep the knife blade straight—not angled—as you cut the soap bar.

6. When you reach the bottom of the soap log, pull the cutting blade away from the log to release the soap slice. Note that because the soap has not yet completely hardened, it may stick to the blade.

7. Gently pull the soap off the blade and place it long-edge-down on a piece of plastic canvas.

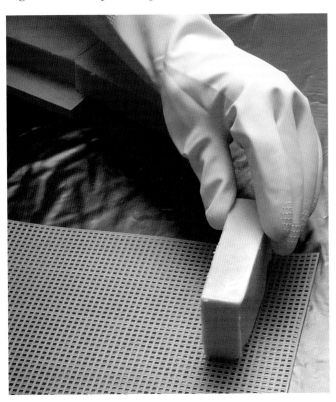

8. Use the same technique to cut a second 1-inch slice off the soap log.

9. Place the second bar next to, but not touching, the first bar.

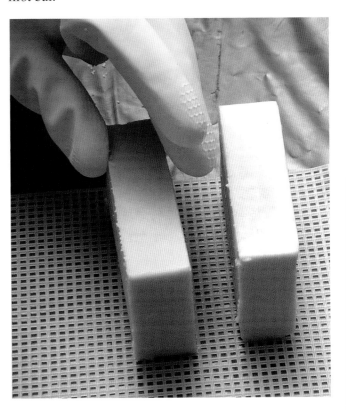

10. Continue in the same manner to cut the entire log into 1-inch bars. Remember to use both hands to push the blade through the soap.

11. Push the blade all the way through to make the last slice. Then, holding the scraper with one hand, grasp the last slice to separate the last two bars. When you are finished, you should have six 1-inch-thick bars of soap (sometimes the last slice may be a little larger or smaller than 1 inch).

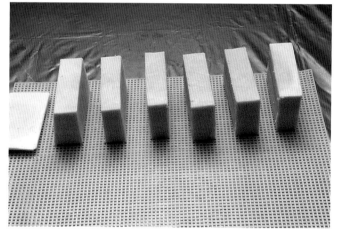

Using a Soap Cutter

If you catch the soap-making bug, a handmade soap cutter, such as this one, will ensure that your bars are all about 1-inch thick. It is specially created to cut soap logs that are 3½ inches wide.

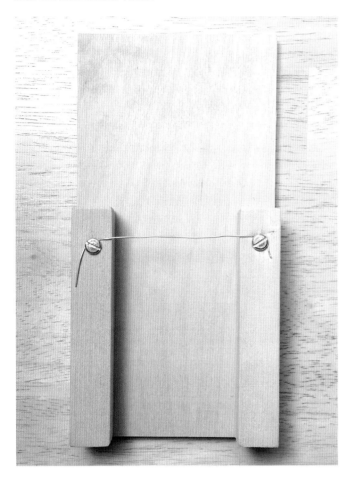

1. To use it, place one of the short ends of your soap log on the cutter base as shown.

2. Grip the guide bars with both hands and place both thumbs low on the log.

3. With steady, even pressure, push the log forward with your thumbs. Continue pushing the bar forward until you have cut all the way through, being careful not to push your thumbs into the cutter wire.

Because the soap has not yet fully hardened, the wire should easily slice through the log.

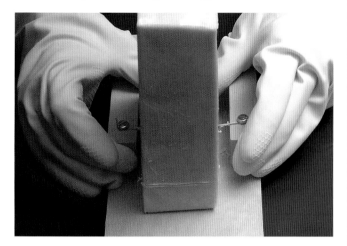

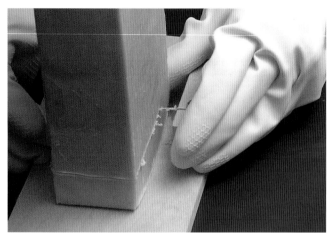

4. Stop pushing the log when the wire has cut all the way through.

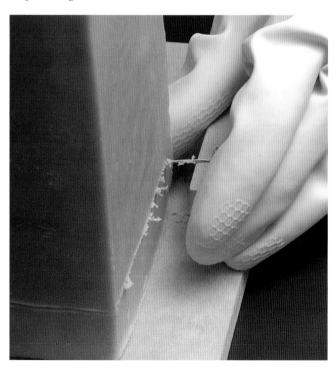

5. To remove the log from the cut slice of soap, grasp the log . . .

. . . slowly twist it to one side . . .

. . . and pull the log away from the soap bar.

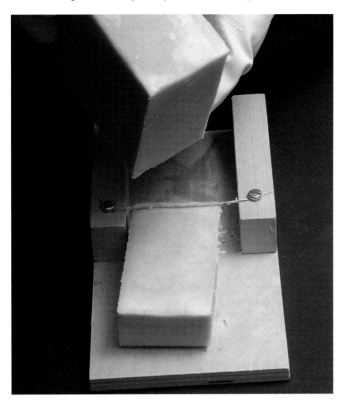

6. Replace the soap log back on the cutter.

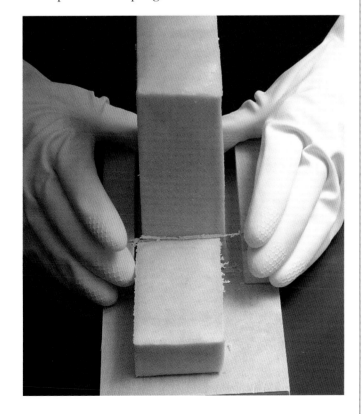

7. Repeat the process of pushing the soap log through the cutting wire.

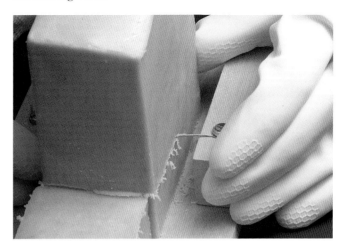

8. Using a twisting motion, remove the log from the cut soap bar.

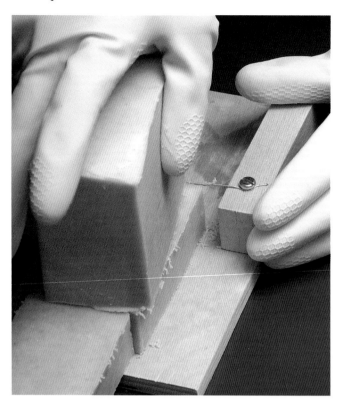

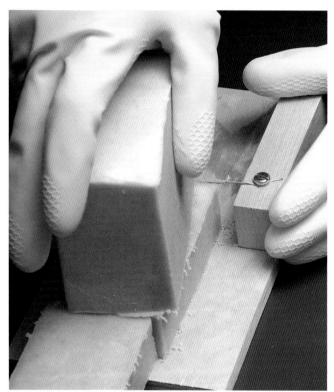

9. Place the soap bars long-edge-down on a piece of plastic canvas or other drying surface.

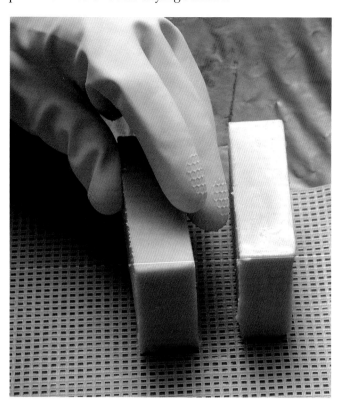

Four soap bars can be cut from a log that was made using a common plastic food container. No liner is necessary when using a plastic mold.

To create a more finished bar, you may want to shave off the uneven edges. Use a kitchen vegetable peeler as shown to take off just a small amount of soap from the long and short edges.

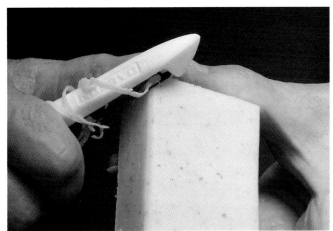

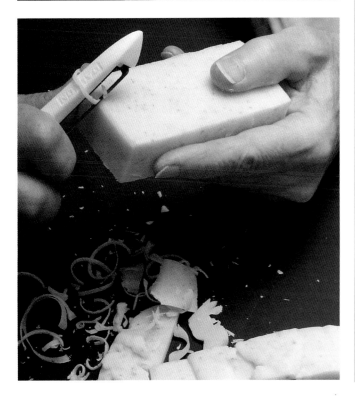

To dry your soap bars, place them out of direct sunlight in a room with low humidity. If water droplets form on the soap surface, the room is too humid. The longer you air dry your soap, the longer it will last when used.

The finished soap is not fully cured and ready to use until it has air dried for about a month.

Finished soap should be kept in an unlidded box or on a tray. Your soap will have a shelf life of about two years.

Congratulations! You've made your first batch of cold process soap. Ready for more? Try these alternative basic recipes to create interesting variations. The possibilities are almost endless, especially when you start adding fragrances, botanicals, and other ingredients. Each of the recipes offered here will result in a soap bar that has its own unique characteristics. To keep track of your favorites, make notes on color, scent, lather, and other soap properties as you create the various soaps. This will help you develop a whole collection of unique soap recipes.

Use the ingredients shown and the cold process instructions to make additional basic recipes. The following recipes fill a 3½-inch wide, 6-inch long, 2½-inch deep mold. To make bigger batches of soap, double or triple the amount of each ingredient.

THREE-OIL SOAP RECIPE #1

3½ ounces coconut oil (100 grams)
8 ounces olive oil (225 grams)
3½ ounces lard (100 grams)
5 ounces distilled water (140 grams)
2 ounces lye (56 grams)

THREE-OIL SOAP RECIPE #2

1 ounce castor oil (28 grams)
7 ounces coconut oil (200 grams)
6 ounces olive oil (170 grams)
5 ounces distilled water (140 grams)
2 ounces lye (56 grams)

THREE-OIL SOAP RECIPE #3

2 ounces castor oil (56 grams)
9 ounces olive oil (250 grams)
6 ounces soybean oil (170 grams)
5 ounces distilled water (140 grams)
2 ounces lye (56 grams)

FOUR-OIL SOAP RECIPE #1

4 ounces coconut oil (112 grams)
4 ounces olive oil (112 grams)
3 ounces safflower oil (84 grams)
4 ounces soybean oil (112 grams)
5 ounces water (140 grams)
2 ounces lye (56 grams)

FOUR-OIL SOAP RECIPE #2

4 ounces canola oil (112 grams)
1 ounce castor oil (28 grams)
8 ounces olive oil (225 grams)
3 ounces soybean oil (84 grams)
5 ounces water (140 grams)
2 ounces lye (56 grams)

3

Soap Additives

The basic cold process recipes produce soap that has a faint aroma, a milky or earthy color, and a smooth surface. You can creatively combine additives to soaps that will produce familiar or exotic scents, subtle or bright colors, and silky smooth or textured surfaces. This chapter will show you how to add some pizzazz to your soap.

41

Colorants

There are many kinds of botanical colorants—spices, seeds, and roots—and clays that you can use to color your soap. When combined with the pale golden color of the oils, the additives will create subtle earth tones, not bright primary colors. (Somewhat brighter colors may be gained by using synthetic pigments and dyes.)

With these colorants, start by using ¼ teaspoon per basic soap recipe batch. If you prefer a darker soap, add more in the next batch you make. Be sure to record the amount you use so that you can duplicate the results.

CINNAMON
Cinnamon is an inexpensive cooking spice that adds fragrance and a dark, earthy brown color to soap.

ANNATTO SEED
This tropical tree seed imparts a yellow-orange color to soap.

TURMERIC
Turmeric is a cooking spice that adds a yellow color.

PAPRIKA
This cooking spice makes a peachy pink bar.

ALKANET
The alkanet root produces shades of pink, blue, and purple, depending on the amount used, types of oil used, and the alkalinity of the soap.

SEA CLAYS
Minerals in rose and green sea clay help remove toxins and impurities from the skin and tighten pores. Use the clay in the color you prefer.

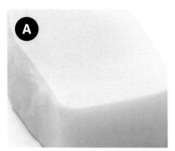   

A. A basic bar of soap without colorants is usually a pale golden color. B. This color was achieved by adding ¼ teaspoon of turmeric. C. A bar enhanced with paprika will have a hint of peachy pink. D. Adding cinnamon will yield a dark, earthy brown color.

Coloring soap using botanicals requires some experimentation to achieve the desired effect. The dramatic difference in these soaps was the result of adding, from left to right, ¼ teaspoon, ½ teaspoon, and 1 full teaspoon of turmeric to a basic soap recipe.

Essential and Fragrance Oils

A big benefit of making your own soap is that you can control the scent. Use individual essential oils to create a citrus, floral, herbal, or minty scent, or combine them for a more complex aroma similar to an expensive perfume. Or you can make scent-free bars if you don't like perfumes or are sensitive to them.

Be sure to use only oils that are cosmetic grade or those made specifically for soap crafting. Essential oils are the concentrated extracted oils from plant leaves, flowers, and berries. A "pure" essential oil is one that does not have any synthetic ingredients. Man-made fragrance oils come in more scents than essential oils and are generally less expensive. Some of these may affect the saponification process, however, and can ruin a batch of cold process soap. That is why it's best to purchase only pure essential oils or fragrance oils from manufacturers that have tested and approved them for soap making.

Scent is subjective, so you will need to experiment with essential and fragrance oils to achieve results that suit you. As a general rule, use about ½ ounce by weight of essential or fragrance oil per one basic soap recipe batch.

Categories of Some Essential and Fragrance Oils

FLORAL
Geranium
Lavender
Lilac
Lily of the Valley
Rose

CITRUS
Grapefruit
Lemon
Lime
Orange

AROMATHERAPY
Lavender
Peppermint
Spearmint
Ylang Ylang

UNIQUE
Musk
Patchouli

MEDICINAL
Tea Tree
Rose Geranium
Lavender
Ylang Ylang

EARTHY
Atlas Cedarwood
Balsam
Bay Laurel
Juniper Berry
Oak Moss
Sandlewood

SEASONAL
Bay Laurel
Peppermint
Pine
Spruce

Skin Conditioners

Soap-supply vendors offer an array of botanicals and oils that can be added to soap to increase its skin-conditioning properties. Some of the most common are listed here.

Aloe vera gel hydrates, heals, and soothes dry skin.

Cinnamon serves as a natural deodorant, although it can be scratchy if used in excess.

Sea clay and other clays remove excess oils from the skin.

Lemon oil helps eliminate bacteria and is a natural deodorant.

Tea tree oil has antiseptic, antifungal, and antiviral properties. It's also an insect repellant, although it can irritate some people's skin.

WHEAT GERM

Wheat germ contains vitamin E and is a natural antioxidant. It exfoliates and cleanses the skin when added as a ground powder. When wheat germ is used in oil form, it makes a mild, conditioning bar. It's available in health food stores and through online vendors.

CALENDULA

Calendula flowers ground to a fine powder help soften rough skin. Whole flowers are added to soap to give it veins of orange and yellow.

LAVENDER

Add ground lavender flowers for a scent that aroma therapists believe reduces anxiety and helps people relax.

OATMEAL

Oatmeal serves as a mild scrubbing agent that helps exfoliate dry skin. Use traditional rolled oats or plain oatmeal—not the instant, flavored kind.

VITAMIN E

Vitamin E can be purchased in liquid form from pharmacies, in the cosmetic areas of discount stores, and through online vendors. Vitamin E also serves as an antioxidant.

COCONUT MILK AND GOAT'S MILK

Coconut milk has been found to have antibacterial and antifungal properties. It can be found in the ethnic foods section of a well-stocked grocery store or in health, organic, or Asian food stores. Once opened, canned coconut milk is usable for only a few days, and it must be refrigerated as it will quickly sour at room temperature.

Add goat's milk to make a moisturizing bar that leaves skin feeling soft and silky. Goat's milk is sold at well-stocked grocery stores and health and organic food stores. Canned milk should be refrigerated after opening. Raw goat's milk can be purchased directly from a goat farm, but it must be kept cold from the time it's purchased until it's used—including the transport time.

Adding Liquids

When adding any liquid—goat's milk, coconut milk, or a water infusion—to soap, you should decrease the amount of water in the initial lye solution by the quantity of liquid you are adding. For example, if you want to add 2 ounces of milk to the basic soap recipe, then reduce the initial amount of water from 5 to 3 ounces. Otherwise, your soap will have too much water and will require a very long drying time. (The same applies to vitamin E oil. Also, if you add more than 2 tablespoons of vitamin E oil to a recipe, you might have to recalculate the SAP values.)

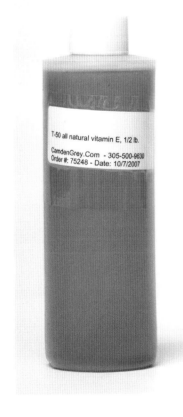

This wonderfully scented oatmeal soap incorporates both color and fragrance. Remember that additions such as these are always added to the basic soap mix when trace is reached. You will need to have all ingredients weighed, measured, and ready to add to the mix before you begin the stirring process.

1. The first step in making this soap is to grind the oatmeal into a powder. Measure 3 heaping tablespoons of rolled oats and put them into a clean electric coffee grinder, or use a mortar and pestle as shown on page 48.

2. Grind the oatmeal flakes to a fine powder.

Ingredient and Equipment List

3 tablespoons rolled oats

⁴⁄₁₀ ounce (by weight) of any scenting oil

Bottle of synthetic colorant of your choice

Mortar and pestle or coffee grinder

Two small bowls to hold measured fragrance and oatmeal

Kitchen measuring spoons

Batch of cold process soap using the basic recipe of your choice

KITCHEN MEASURING SPOONS
Liquids are often measured out in very small quantities.

SMALL BOWLS
Nonaluminum bowls are needed to hold the various ingredients.

MORTAR AND PESTLE OR COFFEE GRINDER
A mortar and pestle can be used to grind oatmeal into a powder. A coffee grinder will work, too.

FRAGRANCE OILS AND COLORANTS
Select an essential or fragrance oil and a liquid colorant. Note that the liquid colorant will not impart a bright color. Brighter colors may be achieved with a powdered oxide colorant, as described on page 57.

A coffee grinder is not essential to prepare oatmeal or other botanicals for soap making. A mortar and pestle will do just fine. To use this tool, start by placing the oatmeal in the mortar bowl. Press down on the flakes repeatedly with the pestle to break them down. Then use a circular motion to press the oatmeal against the side of the mortar. It should take only a few minutes of grinding to produce a fine textured powder for use in your soap. You can use the same procedure to prepare seeds and dried flowers.

3. Pour $\frac{4}{10}$ ounce of cosmetic-grade fragrance oil into a small bowl. (If the scent of the finished soap is too strong or not strong enough to suit you, make a note and adjust your recipe the next time.)

Some soap makers like to match the color of the soap to the fragrance: purple for lavender, green for bayberry, pink for rose, and so on. Use colorant formulated for soap making. The powdered form will result in brighter colors than the liquid form. *Food coloring will not work well in the cold process method of soap making and so should not be used.*

Remember that the oatmeal, fragrance, and colorant are added to the basic soap mixture when it reaches trace stage.

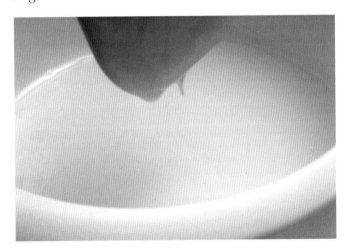

4. Liquid colorant is packaged in plastic bottles with a dropper tip. To add bottled colorant at trace stage, squeeze the bottle gently to release the colorant one drop at a time. Scatter about twelve drops on the surface of the soap.

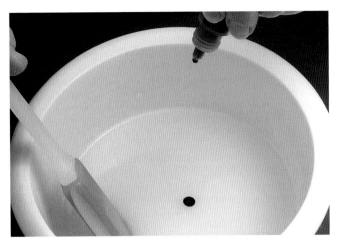

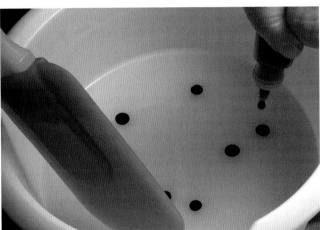

5. Gently blend the color into the soap mixture. If it isn't dark enough, add three or four more drops, then stir them in until the mix is of a uniform color. Repeat as desired.

6. Stir gently until the colorant is completely blended into the soap mix. Keep in mind that even when colorant is added, cold process soap will always have a somewhat natural, earthy appearance.

7. Pour the fragrance oil into the soap mixture and use your spatula to blend it in thoroughly.

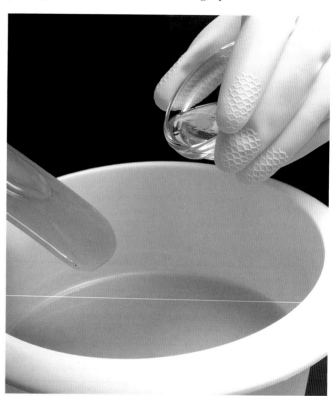

8. Just as you would add flour to a cake mix, add the powdered oatmeal a little at a time while stirring continuously.

9. Add and stir until the oatmeal is completely incorporated into the mixture.

10. When all the additives are incorporated, gently pour the soap mixture into the mold, being careful not to splash or create air bubbles. Push the liquid into the mold with the spatula. Set the bowl, spatula, and other equipment aside for 24 hours before cleaning.

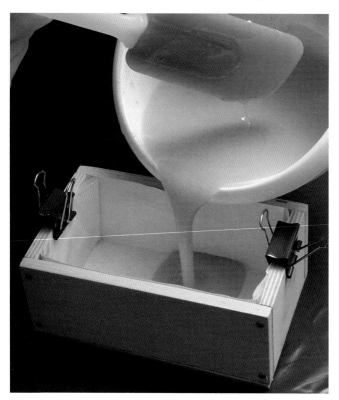

11. Cover the mold with two towels to put it to bed.

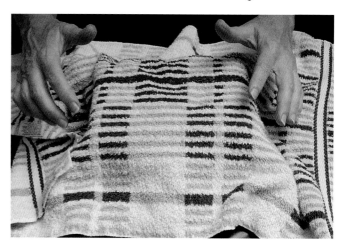

Your finished oatmeal soap bars will exfoliate and moisturize dry skin. Notice that the liquid purple color creates a muted tone.

Making this colorful soap is a great way to combine a bar of colored and uncolored basic soap to create something that's completely different. The colored soap used here features added cinnamon, which—like all additives—is mixed into a basic soap mixture at trace stage.

Start with a colored bar of basic soap that has cured for a couple of days, but less than a week, so it is still somewhat soft. Cinnamon was used to give this bar its dark brown color, which contrasts nicely with the uncolored basic soap recipe and will create the interesting two-tone effect.

Equipment and Ingredient List

Safety gear and all equipment to make cold process soap

Ingredients to make one batch of one of the basic soap recipes

One bar of colored basic soap that has cured no more than a week

1. Use your board scraper/slicer or a sharp knife to cut the colored soap into nuggets that are about ¾ inch by ¼ inch. Set the nuggets aside.

2. Make a batch of basic soap following the instructions in chapter 2.

3. When the basic soap mixture reaches the trace stage, begin adding the colored soap nuggets.

4. Stir gently as you slowly add the nuggets.

5. Stir until all the nuggets are incorporated into the mix.

6. Then pour the mixture into a mold, being careful not to splash. Use your spatula to scrape all of the mixture into the mold.

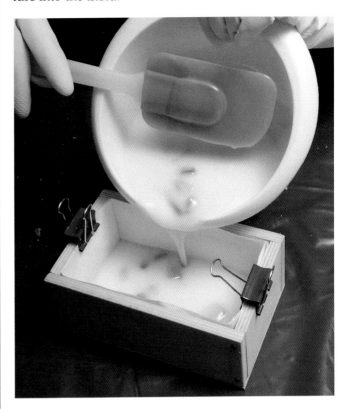

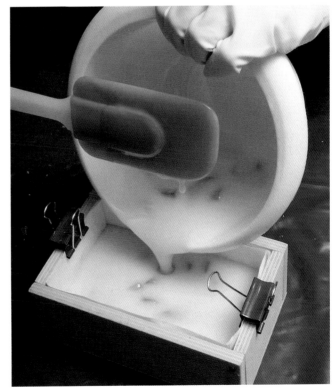

7. Follow the basic soap-making process to put your soap to bed—put the lid on the mold and wrap it with two layers of towels and blankets. Wait overnight to clean up the bowl and utensils. Unmold the two-tone soap after 24 hours.

8. Once you have mastered the basic soap recipes, try experimenting to create a variety of two-tone soaps. You may want to try using smaller pieces of a contrasting colored soap or soap shavings instead of the larger nuggets.

Finished two-tone soap bars are ready for gift giving.

Powdered oxide colorants produce bright colors in cold process soap. The recipe used to illustrate the process of making a batch of swirled and layered soap follows. The same procedure may be used with any basic soap recipe provided in this book.

The following recipe will fill a mold that is 3½ inches wide, 12 inches long, and 3 inches deep. If you wish to experiment with different quantities of soap, adjust the colorant mixture accordingly.

Seven-Oil Soap Recipe

10 ounces water (280 grams)
5.8 ounces lye (164 grams)
7 ounces coconut oil (200 grams)
7 ounces palm kernel oil (200 grams)
7 ounces palm oil (200 grams)
2 ounces castor oil (58 grams)
7 ounces olive oil (200 grams)
7 ounces soybean oil (200 grams)
5 ounces sunflower oil (140 grams)
1 ounce scent of choice (28 grams)
1 teaspoon powdered oxide colorant of choice
3 teaspoons glycerin

Soap with Colored Swirls

Ingredients

Seven-oil recipe or basic soap recipe of choice to fill a mold that is 3½ inches wide, 12 inches long, and 3 inches deep. (This is twice the volume of the basic soap recipes.)

1 teaspoon powdered oxide colorant of choice
   (Use more or less to desired intensity.)
3 teaspoons liquid glycerin
1 ounce fragrance oil
   (Use more or less to desired strength.)

Powdered oxide colorants are available from soap making suppliers and online vendors.

Glycerin is sold at most pharmacies, in craft stores, and on internet sites. It is a colorless liquid that blends with both oil and water, making it an excellent medium in which to incorporate the dry powdered color into the soap base.

Safety Note: Protect yourself from inhaling powdered colorant dust by wearing a face mask.

1. Prior to making the soap, prepare the colorant by combining 1 teaspoon of oxide powder with 3 teaspoons glycerin in a small bowl. It takes about 1 minute to thoroughly blend the color and glycerin by stirring with a spoon. This should be done at least 24 hours in advance in order to fully hydrate the dry powder colorant.

Better color swirl results will be achieved if you make two or more batches of soap at a time. If you wish to experiment with a single batch, reduce the amount of oxide colorant to ¼ teaspoon and glycerin to 1½ teaspoons.

2. Make either the seven-oil recipe or other cold process soap recipe by combining oils and stirring to combine . . .

. . . adding the lye and water solution and stirring to combine . . .

. . . and stirring to trace when mixture becomes thick, opaque in color, and falls slowly off the spoon.

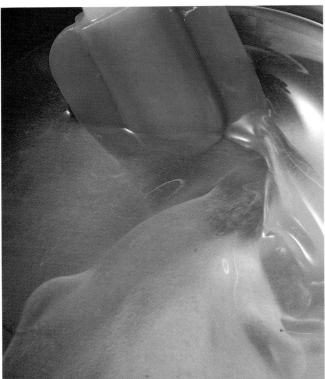

3. If desired, add 1 ounce of fragrance oil at this time and stir just until blended.

4. Place a clean 1-quart plastic container on the scale and tare it. Pour 4 ounces of soap into the container and remove from the scale.

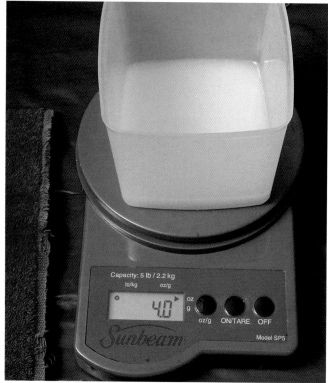

5. Using a spoon, add the colorant/glycerin mixture to the soap in the container.

6. Use an immersion blender set on low in 2-second bursts to completely mix the colorant mixture into the soap mixture.

7. Drizzle the color mixture onto the surface of the soap mixture.

8. Pull a spatula through the soap mixture two or three times to create a swirl pattern. *Do not stir*—if stirred, the mixture will become a solid color.

9. Gently pour the mixture into the mold. If necessary, use a spatula to smooth the surface of the soap.

10. Put the soap to bed. After the soap has set for at least 24 hours, follow the steps for unmolding and cutting as illustrated in the basic soap-making process.

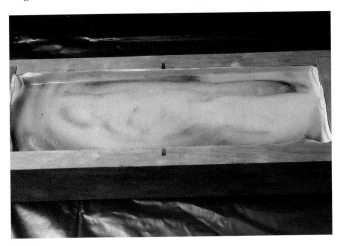

The swirl patterns will vary from bar to bar and batch to batch as these purple and green samples show.

Layered Soap

Ingredients

Seven-oil recipe or basic soap recipe of choice to fill a mold that is 3½ inches wide, 12 inches long, and 3 inches deep. (Note that this is twice the volume of the basic soap recipes.)

1 teaspoon of green powdered oxide
   (or color of choice)
1 teaspoon of yellow powdered oxide
   (or color of choice)
1 teaspoon of blue powdered oxide
   (or color of choice)
9 teaspoons liquid glycerin (3 teaspoons per color)
1 ounce fragrance oil, if desired
   (Use more or less to desired strength.)
Two clean 1-quart plastic containers

1. Prior to making your chosen soap recipe, prepare three color solutions. This should be done at least 24 hours in advance to fully hydrate the dry powder colorant.

2. Combine 1 teaspoon of yellow oxide powder with 3 teaspoons glycerin in small bowl. It takes about 1 minute to thoroughly blend color and glycerin by stirring with a spoon.

3. In a separate bowl, mix 1 teaspoon green colorant with 3 teaspoons glycerin until thoroughly blended. In a third bowl, mix 1 teaspoon blue colorant with 3 teaspoons glycerin in the same way. Allow the three colors to sit overnight so that the color is fully hydrated.

4. Make either the seven-oil or other cold process soap recipe (that has been doubled) by combining oils and stirring to combine . . .

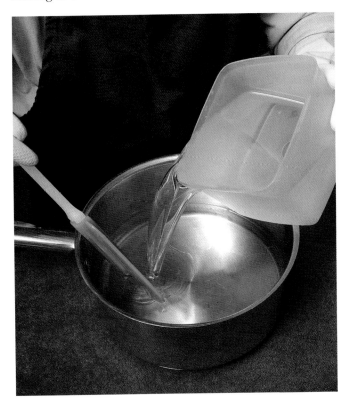

. . . adding the lye and water solution and stirring to combine . . .

. . . and stirring with an immersion blender and spoon until the mixture reaches trace stage.

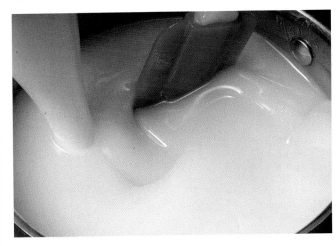

5. If desired, add 1 ounce of fragrance oil at this time and stir just until blended.

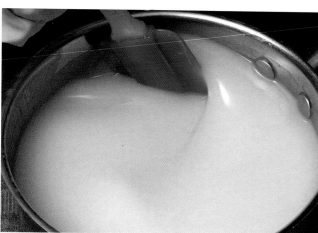

6. Place a 1-quart plastic container on the scale and tare it. Pour 19 ounces of soap (a third of the mixture) into the container and remove from the scale.

7. Place a second 1-quart plastic container on the scale and tare it. Pour 19 more ounces of soap (about half of the remaining mixture) into the second container and remove from the scale.

8. Add yellow colorant to a soap mixture in one of the quart containers and stir with a spoon or immersion blender set on low in 2-second bursts to thoroughly combine.

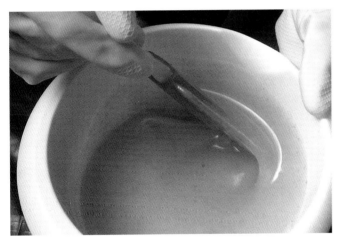

9. Pour the yellow soap evenly into the mold. Smooth the surface with a spatula.

10. Add green colorant to the soap mixture in the second container and stir with a spoon or immersion blender set on low in 2-second bursts to thoroughly combine.

11. Using the back of a large spoon or a spatula to break the fall of the liquid, slowly pour the green soap on top of the yellow. This will help prevent the two color layers from combining. Pour evenly over the length of the mold. Smooth the surface with a spatula.

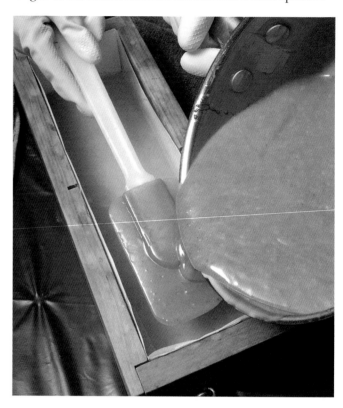

12. Add blue colorant to the soap mixture in the last container and stir with a spoon or immersion blender set on low in 2-second bursts to thoroughly combine.

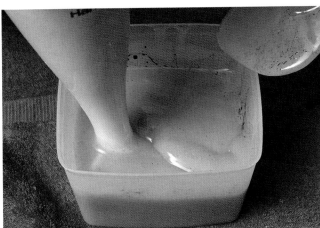

13. Slowly and evenly pour the blue soap on top of the green over the length of the mold using the back of a large spoon or a spatula to break the fall.

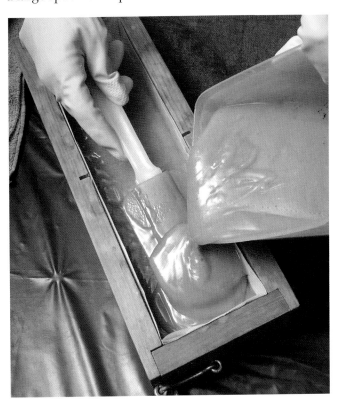

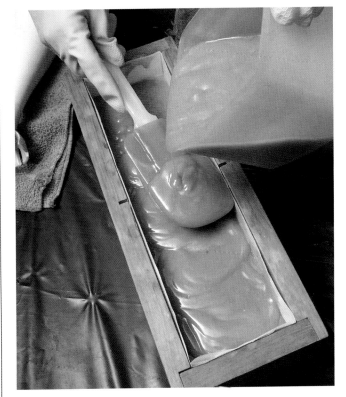

14. Smooth the surface with a spatula.

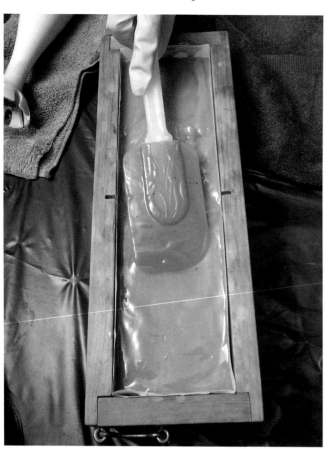

15. Put the soap to bed. After the soap has set for at least 24 hours, you can unmold and cut the soap.

Notice how the color layers sink slightly into each other, providing an interesting appearance.

Mixing Your Own Colors

If you find that you don't have the exact soap color you need, try mixing your own. Powdered oxide colorants can be combined to create different colors. Yellow and blue makes green, red and blue makes purple, yellow and red makes orange, and so on. When mixing colors, start with the lighter color first and blend the darker color into it.

1. To make a rich, solid green, for example, place 1 teaspoon of yellow oxide colorant in a small bowl and add 3 ounces of glycerin. Stir until completely blended.

2. Add to this 1 teaspoon of blue colorant and stir until the color is a uniform green.

3. To darken the color, add another teaspoon of blue and another teaspoon of glycerin and stir. The result is a rich green color.

This recipe uses a full 12-ounce can of evaporated goat's milk and fills a mold that is 10½ inches wide by 12 inches long by 3½ inches deep. (Note that this is six times the amount of the basic soap recipes. You can change the amount of soap to be made by adjusting each ingredient in the recipe accordingly.)

1. Prepare the ingredients. Carefully weigh all oils as instructed in the cold process soap-making procedure. Combine them in an 8-quart stainless steel stockpot or large plastic bowl of similar size.

2. To the oils, add the lye and water solution that has been cooled to about 100 degrees F.

Recipe

Note that all ingredients should be measured by weight, except for the goat's milk, which is a liquid measure, and the oatmeal, which is a dry measure.

20 ounces water (565 grams)
15.9 ounces lye (450 grams)
21 ounces coconut oil (600 grams)
21 ounces palm oil (600 grams)
21 ounces lard (600 grams)
7 ounces almond oil (200 grams)
7 ounces castor oil (200 grams)
14 ounces grapeseed oil (400 grams)
21 ounces olive oil (600 grams)
7 ounces sunflower oil (200 grams)
1 12-ounce can evaporated goat's milk
3 ounces lavender essential oil (85 grams)
1 cup of finely ground oatmeal

3. Gently stir the oil, lye, and water mixture to combine all the ingredients. Then, using an immersion blender on the low setting, mix thoroughly for about 2 minutes.

Soap Additives

73

4. Shake the can of evaporated goat's milk prior to use. Add 12 fluid ounces (liquid measure) of evaporated goat's milk to the soap mixture.

5. Use an immersion blender set on low for about 15 seconds to thoroughly incorporate the goat's milk. Rather than stirring to trace for this recipe, add the oatmeal at this point. As you add the oatmeal, the mixture will thicken to the proper consistency for adding the fragrance oil.

6. Gradually add 1 cup of ground oatmeal while continually stirring with a spoon or spatula until all the oatmeal is incorporated.

Adding oatmeal a little at a time will help prevent it from clumping in the soap mixture.

7. Add fragrance oil and stir until thoroughly incorporated.

8. Pour soap mixture into the mold.

9. Smooth the surface of the soap with a spatula.

10. Put the soap to bed. After the soap has cooled completely, unmold and cut into bars as instructed in the cold process soap-making procedure.

4

Rebatching

Nothing beats the feel of lathering up with a large, homemade bar of cold process soap. You may decide, however, that you want to offer homemade soaps as gifts or party favors, so a smaller size and a fun, fancy shape might be more suitable. You can easily create such soaps by remelting soap bars you've made before they've fully cured or hardened. This process of "rebatching" soap is made simple by using a microwave oven. You can even save your soap scraps and shape them into balls for use at home.

These molded soaps also feature an oil infusion that adds a swirl of color. The oil-infusion method can be used to add a variety of botanical colors to your soap.

For the basic mixture in this recipe, we'll use cold process soap bars that have cured for a few days but no longer than a week. In this particular recipe, we'll use an infusion of annatto seeds to achieve an orange swirl pattern, but you can use other botanicals or colorants to get the results you want.

Equipment and Supplies List

Any shape of plastic soap mold
Cutting board or other counter-surface protector
Sharp knife for cutting soap into small pieces
Kitchen grater or electric food chopper/grater
Handheld vegetable peeler
Small kitchen food strainer
Small plastic mixing bowl
Small bowl to make color infusion
Plastic or silicon spatula
Microwave oven

MICROWAVE OVEN
Microwaving allows you to soften soap and heat oil quickly. You must be careful, however, that things don't get too hot too fast. Never leave a microwave unattended while it is in use.

STRAINER
A small kitchen strainer helps separate botanicals from the infused oil after it has been heated.

KITCHEN GRATER OR ELECTRIC CHOPPER
A simple kitchen grater or electric chopper will prepare already-made soap for rebatching.

Ingredient List

Three bars of basic cold process soap
1 tablespoon of annatto seeds
2 tablespoons of grapeseed oil
Distilled water

BASIC RECIPE SOAP BARS

Three basic recipe soap bars measuring about 3½ inches by 2¼ inches by 1 inch will be used for the rebatching process.

PLASTIC MOLDS

Fancy plastic molds designed for making poured soap or candy come in a wide range of geometric and figure shapes, such as flowers, seashells, stars, hearts, and many others. They can be reused many times.

ANNATTO SEEDS

In an infusion, these tropical tree seeds impart an orange or golden yellow color to oil. The seeds can be found in Latin food markets, the Latin section of supermarkets, or online.

GRAPESEED OIL

This oil can be heated to a relatively high temperature without smoking.

The Oil-Infusion Method

When you pour hot water over a tea bag, you are making an infusion. In soap making, dried or fresh flowers, herbs, or seeds are added to a small quantity of oil and heated to release the color into the oil.

The longer the mixture sits, or "steeps," the stronger the color will become. When the infusion is sufficiently strong, separate the liquid from the solids using a kitchen food strainer. Add 1 or 2 teaspoons of the liquid infusion per batch to a basic soap recipe when it reaches trace.

Remember to always be cautious when heating oil, as it will smoke and burn if the temperature gets too high. Never heat oil on the stovetop or in a microwave unattended.

1. The first step in preparing an oil infusion is to measure out 1 tablespoon of annatto seeds into a small bowl. Then add about 2 tablespoons of grapeseed oil (an exact measurement is not critical here).

2. Microwave the seed and oil mixture for 20 seconds on full power. Remove the mixture from the microwave and let it cool for a minute. Then microwave it again for 20 seconds on full power. After the second heating, the oil should be a dark red-orange color. Set the infusion aside to cool.

Rebatching

Grating the Soap

1. Start by grating three bars of soap with either a kitchen grater or an electric food chopper. With a kitchen grater, grate the soap bars as you would cheese. Place a cutting board under the grater and use the side of the grater that has the largest openings. Grip the soap bar tightly and rub it against the grater teeth with a downward motion. When you have only a small piece of ungrated soap remaining, use a kitchen knife to cut it into shaving-sized pieces.

2. Place the shavings in a microwavable bowl.

You can also use an electric food chopper to grate the soap bars for rebatching.

1. First use a kitchen knife to cut the bars of soap into pieces that will fit into the chopper's hopper.

2. Follow the manufacturer's instructions for using the grater attachment. Place small pieces of soap into the hopper and place the pusher over the pieces. Turn on the grater and shoot the shavings into a microwave-safe bowl.

3. Continue shaving all three bars of cold process soap.

Rebatching the Soap

1. Add ¼ cup of distilled water to the soap shavings.

2. Blend slightly to distribute the water evenly throughout.

3. Microwave the soap shavings for 1 minute at 70 percent power.

4. Remove the bowl and stir gently. The shavings should be warm but not liquefied.

5. Retrieve the cooled bowl of infused oil. Tilt the bowl to one side and use a teaspoon to scoop up the oil, leaving the solids behind.

6. Scatter drops of the infused oil on top of the softened soap shavings.

7. Stir the colored infusion throughout the shavings.

8. Place the bowl in the microwave and heat for 10 seconds at 50 percent power.

Don't be alarmed to see the soap rise and foam up as it is being heated.

Be careful when removing the bowl, as it and the shavings will be very hot.

The resulting mix will resemble cheesy mashed potatoes.

9. Stir the mix until the color is evenly distributed throughout.

10. Use the spreader to fill your mold with the mixture.

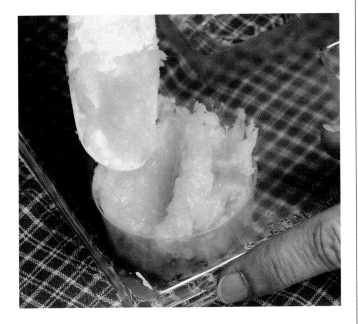

11. Level off the top of the mold.

12. Tap the mold lightly on the table to eliminate any air bubbles.

13. If necessary, level the top of the mold again.

14. To make a darker mixture, use the remaining annatto seed infusion. Microwave the infusion for 10 seconds on high power.

15. Transfer 1 teaspoon of the oil and annatto seeds into a small strainer held over the soap mixture, which will allow the oil to flow through.

16. Use the spreader to thoroughly mix the color into the mixture.

17. If you want the color to be even stronger, repeat the process of microwaving the infusion, spooning a teaspoon of the stronger oil infusion through a strainer into the soap mixture, and stirring.

18. If your soap mixture becomes too thick to work with, add 1 tablespoon of distilled water, microwave in 10-second increments, and stir.

19. Carefully remove the soap mixture from the microwave—it will be hot.

20. Stir the mix until the colorant is thoroughly incorporated into the soap.

21. Use your spreader to fill the mold.

22. Continue filling the mold until the mixture reaches the top and level it off as before. Tap the mold gently on the table to dislodge any air bubbles.

23. You do not need to wait long to remove the soap from the mold. After several hours, check the soap to see if it is cool and hard.

24. If it is, it's ready to be unmolded. Grasp the side of the mold with one hand, and with the thumb of the other hand, gently press down on the soap. Repeat for all of the soaps in the mold you are using.

25. Once all the soaps are released, simply lift the mold up and off the soap.

26. Use a vegetable peeler to trim the rough edges.

The color of the bottom soap—the result of the first infusion made with the annatto seed—is almost imperceptible. The stronger colors of the middle and top soaps are the result of the second and third infusions.

91

This colorful soap is made by adding colorant to a portion of a rebatched mixture, which is then swirled into the uncolored portion.

1. Start with three bars of basic recipe soap that have been shaved and heated in the microwave about 1 minute at 70 percent power to soften them.

2. Add the color intensity of the infusion you prefer to about a third of the soap mixture.

3. Allow the colored soap to cool, then use your spreader to gather up about 1 tablespoon of mixture.

4. Drop the colored mixture onto the surface of the uncolored mix.

5. Continue until you have six colored soap globs spread out on the surface of the uncolored mix.

6. Use your spreader to swirl the colored soap into the uncolored soap. Do not overstir or the soap will become a solid yellow.

7. If the soap becomes too thick to work with, heat it in 10-second increments in the microwave on high power.

8. Use your spreader to make an X shape through the soap.

This will further distribute the colored soap in an uneven pattern.

Rebatching

9. Fill the soap mold with the mixture.

10. Use your spreader to smooth out the top of the soap.

11. Tap the mold gently on the table to release any air bubbles that may have formed.

12. Allow to cool. Unmold and finish the edges as shown on page 91.

Once you have a sufficient amount of soap bits, you can recycle them by making soap balls using a slow cooker. If the soap scraps are very dry to the touch, you should moisten them with water. Sprinkle a few drops at a time and toss lightly until the scraps are pliable. (You may need to use up to several ounces of water if you have a large quantity of scraps.) Let the scraps sit for 12 to 24 hours so the moisture is fully absorbed. Be careful not to add too much water, as that would result in the soap balls taking a very long time to thoroughly dry.

1. Warm the soap bits on low heat until the soap is slightly melted. The soap is ready when it turns a golden color and the oils are just starting to liquefy. Watch the pot, however, because the soap can burn and stick to the sides if the cooker gets too hot.

Rebatching

2. With your hands protected with rubber kitchen gloves, use a spoon to scoop out a palm-sized portion of the warmed soap. The oils in the soap can get very hot, so test the temperature before handling it.

3. Press the soap between your palms and gently mold it into a ball. The warm soap balls will be gooey, so place them on a plate or tray.

4. Let the balls cool until the oils resolidify, but before the balls have fully hardened. Then press each ball between your palms, turning as you press to form uniform, rounded shapes.

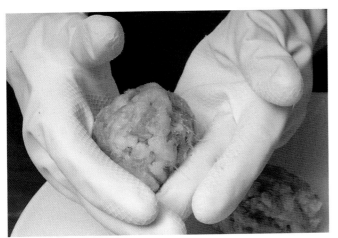

As the resulting soap balls are a random combination of oils, fragrances, and colors, they are generally used at home rather than given as gifts.

Rebatching

5

Creating Your Own Soap Recipes

Using the basic recipes as foundations, you can change things around to create soap bars that have their own unique characteristics. To keep track of your favorites, keep notes on color, scent, lather, and whatever other soap properties you desire. Once you've mastered the basics, you can move on to creating custom recipes using your own combination of oils.

THE OIL PHASE

The main ingredient in soap is oil, and the process of soap making is called saponification, in which the oils combine with lye (sodium hydroxide) to make soap. The end product contains saponified oils.

Soap can be made with any animal or vegetable oil. Each oil has a saponification value or "SAP value." This

simply means that it takes the SAP value amount of lye to saponify one unit of oil. Whether you are using grams, ounces, or pounds, each unit must be multiplied by the SAP value to achieve the proper amount of lye to saponify the oil.

The soap recipes provided here are made with oils that are readily available at almost any grocery store. After you make these and become acquainted with the soap-making process, you might want to consider using other oils that are available—almost any edible oil can be used to make soap.

You can develop your own recipes, or you can take one of the recipes included in this book and just replace one of the listed oils with an alternative oil. But because each oil has a unique SAP value, you will need to recal-

BASIC OIL CHART

These oils are relatively inexpensive and generally available at grocery stores. Membership warehouse stores and food discount stores may offer a better value if you want to buy large quantities. Lard can also be found in grocery stores, stores specializing in organic products, and farm markets. (Tallow makes wonderful soap but requires more work—before using it in soap, it must be rendered, which is the process of melting and straining out the beef fat.)

Oil/Fat	Creates hard bar	Creates fluffy lather	Creates stable lather	Creates conditioning bar
Canola Oil			X	X
Castor Oil			X	X
Coconut Oil	X	X		
Corn Oil			X	X
Lard	X		X	X
Olive Oil			X	X
Palm Kernel Oil	X	X		
Palm Oil	X		X	
Peanut Oil			X	X
Rice Bran Oil	X	X		
Safflower Oil			X	X
Soybean Oil			X	X
Sunflower Oil			X	X
Tallow	X		X	X

culate the proper amount of lye and water to use in the revised recipe. Refer to the saponification chart provided on page 101 to make these calculations.

By using different oils in a recipe, you will start to discover how oils change the properties and appeal of the finished soap. Experiment with different combinations of various oils, and you will soon find that you have created your own personal ultimate soap.

THE WATER PHASE
At one time, soap was made with rainwater, but impurities in rainwater make it undesirable as a soap ingredient. Public water supplies also include chemicals such as chlorine, chloramines, and fluoride, and water from private wells may contain minerals that could affect the quality of your soap. For all these reasons, distilled water is the preferred choice for soap making. Reasonably priced bottled distilled water is readily available in most grocery stores.

The amount of water required for a particular batch of soap is based on the amount of lye included. In general, to calculate how much water is necessary to make your soap, multiply the weight of the lye by 2.5 to get the weight of water to be used. This is the mathematical formula: $Lye \times 2.5 = H_2O$.

All recipes in this book are based on the 2.5 calculation. The 2.5 value is somewhat flexible, however. You may choose to use more or less, but remember that you must have enough water to dissolve the lye. Do not go below a multiplication factor of 2.0 or you may end up with undissolved pockets of lye in your soap.

If you use less water, the lye solution will be stronger, and the chemical reaction between the oils and the lye will be faster. If you use more water, the lye solution will be weaker, and you will have more time to watch the chemical reaction and get to understand the soap-making process.

LUXURY OIL CHART

Indulge yourself with silky-smooth soap made with luxury oils. As the chart shows, these oils will ensure that your soap lathers well and has top conditioning properties. These oils are a bit pricier than the basic oils. Some are available at grocery stores, while others may be found at pharmacies, health food stores, and herbal shops, or through online vendors.

Oil/Fat	Contributes to a firm soap	Helps make a stable lather	Contributes to a conditioning soap
Almond Oil		X	X
Apricot Kernal Oil		X	X
Borage Oil		X	X
Calendula Oil		X	X
Cocoa Butter	X	X	X
Evening Primrose Oil		X	
Hazelnut Oil		X	X
Hemp Seed Oil		X	X
Jojoba Oil		X	X
Kukui Nut Oil		X	X
Lanolin	X		X
Macadamia Nut Oil		X	X
Neem Oil		X	X
Sesame Oil		X	X
Shea Butter	X	X	X
Wheat germ Oil		X	X

Until you are very familiar with soap making, you may be more comfortable using a larger quantity of water.

DETERMINING LYE AMOUNTS

To determine the amount of lye needed for a recipe, multiply the amount of oil you are using (in weight, not volume) by the SAP value for that particular oil. If you are using a combination of oils, multiply each oil by its SAP value and add all the amounts together to get the total amount of lye necessary for saponification.

Example 1. If you are using 32 ounces of olive oil, multiply that amount by 0.135 (olive oil's SAP value) to get 4.32 ounces of lye needed.

Example 2. If you are using 32 ounces of olive oil and 10 ounces of hazelnut oil, multiply 32 by 0.135 (olive oil's SAP value) and 10 by 0.136 (hazelnut's SAP

value) to get 4.32 and 1.36, which added together comes to 5.68 ounces of lye needed.

DON'T FORGET ABOUT "SUPERFATTING"

Making soap that has an exact oil-to-lye ratio—soap that has just enough lye to cause saponification of all the oil and fat in the mixture—would result in a harsh, drying bar. "Superfatting" a mixture ensures that there will be "extra" oil and fat in the soap after saponification. This is done by calculating a percentage of oil over and above the SAP value. A "superfatting" range between 5 and 10 percent is generally accepted as satisfactory (all the recipes offered in this book have a built-in superfat factor of 8 percent).

When making your own recipes, keep in mind that the higher the percentage of oil—a more superfatted blend—the softer the soap will be. A softer soap is

SAPONIFICATION (SAP) VALUE CHART

Fat or Oil	Lye (NaOH), in ounces
Almond Oil	0.136
Apricot Kernel Oil	0.137
Avocado Oil	0.133
Borage Oil	0.133
Canola Oil	0.132
Castor Oil	0.128
Cocoa Butter	0.137
Coconut Oil	0.191
Corn Oil	0.136
Evening Primrose Oil	0.136
Hazelnut Oil	0.136
Hempseed Oil	0.135
Jojoba Oil	0.069
Kukui Nut Oil	0.135
Lanolin	0.074
Lard	0.139
Macadamia Nut Oil	0.139
Neem Oil	0.137
Olive Oil	0.135
Palm Kernel Oil	0.177
Palm Oil	0.142
Peanut Oil	0.136
Rapeseed Oil	0.132
Safflower Oil,	0.137
Sesame Oil	0.133
Shea Butter	0.129
Soybean Oil	0.136
Sunflower Seed Oil	0.136
Tallow, Beef	0.141
Walnut Oil	0.135
Wheat Germ Oil	0.132

DETERMINING FINAL WATER AMOUNTS

Ounces/Oil	SAP Value	Lye
8 ounces coconut oil	0.191	1.53
8 ounces soybean oil (vegetable shortening)	0.136	1.09
15 ounces olive oil	0.135	2.03
1 ounce castor oil	0.128	0.13
Lye		**4.78**
6% Superfatting Calculation	4.78 x 0.94 = 4.49 oz. lye	
Water Calculation	4.49 x 2.5 = 11.2 oz. water	

milder on the skin, but it will dissolve faster when used. A balance needs to be reached when developing a recipe so that the resulting soap is mild yet hard enough to be long lasting.

You might find that you prefer a soap superfatted at 6 or 9 percent. Careful record keeping as you make soap will allow you to adjust the amounts of lye, oil, and water when you make subsequent batches.

Adjusting Lye Amounts to Superfat Soap

To superfat your own recipes at 8 percent, you must reduce the amount of lye used in the recipe. This is most easily accomplished by multiplying the amount of lye needed by the complement of 8 percent (the complement is 100 percent minus 8 percent, equaling 92 percent—or 0.92). Thus, in Example 1, which calls for 4.32 ounces of lye, you superfat the recipe at 8 percent by multiplying 4.32 by 0.92 to get 3.97 ounces of lye.

Example 2 would require 5.22 ounces of lye for a superfat percentage of 8 (5.68 x 0.92 = 5.22).

DETERMINING FINAL WATER AMOUNTS

To determine the amount of water needed for a recipe, multiply the amount of lye by 2.5. So in Example 1, 3.97 ounces of lye multiplied by 2.5 comes to 9.92 ounces of water. In Example 2, 5.22 ounces of lye multiplied by 2.5 comes to 13.05 ounces of water.

As your soap dries, there will be some evaporation of water. The final batch, when cut into bars, will not have the same total weight as the batch did before drying.

6
Packaging Finished Soap

Creatively packaging your soap will help make it a much-appreciated gift or party favor. There are as many simple and inexpensive ways to package and present your soap as there are recipes. Here are some ideas to get you started:

Tie your soap with string and tuck in a few sprigs of lavender or other flowers.

CLEAR BAGS

Craft stores and kitchen shops stock clear candy bags. Place a soap bar into one of the 3¾-inch by 6-inch bags and tie with a curled ribbon that matches the theme colors of a special event or holiday. The bag will protect the soap if the gift is to be used in a gift basket or as a stocking stuffer.

"CIGAR BANDS"

Cut a sheet of 8½-inch by 11-inch cardstock (available at craft and office supply stores) into 2-inch by 8½-inch strips. Wrap around the soap and secure on the bottom with cellophane tape, all-purpose white glue, or rubber cement. Use a pen or marker to identify the soap, or handwrite a personal message.

Using the Computer. If you want to use a computer to create your message, select the 8½-inch by 11-inch paper size setting and set the top and bottom margins at ½-inch. Create a 1½-inch by 1½-inch text box. Type your message in the box and add clip art if you wish. Copy and paste the text box so that you have five boxes. Center the text boxes from right to left and top to bottom and print. Cut into 2-inch by 8½-inch strips. Wrap the strips around the soap and secure on the bottom with tape, white glue, or rubber cement.

FABRIC RIBBON WRAP

Here's a good way to use up those fabric or ribbon scraps. Cut or tear a 1-inch wide, 40-inch long strip of fabric or fabric ribbon. Wrap the soap as you would a present and tie a simple bow. Cotton fabric with calico or country prints, or grosgrain ribbon, complement the handmade soap. For a more formal appearance, use wire-edge taffeta, satin, or organza. A variety of ribbons can be found at fabric and craft stores.

Pair your gift with a glass or pottery soap dish.

103

MAKING A CUSTOM SOAP BOX

The paper box pattern on page 105 is the perfect size for a bar of handmade soap. For the purpose of illustration, the fold lines were printed on the decorative side of the box. When making your box, print the box template on the wrong side of the paper. The design shown below was made with real flowers and leaves using a computer scanner.

Follow these steps to make your own custom soap gift box:

1. Copy or trace the pattern onto a piece of card stock or construction paper.
2. To decorate the box, do one of the following:
- Use all-purpose white paper glue or rubber cement to glue gift wrap to the side of the paper that does not include the box template.
- Use computer clip art to create a custom design or fill the computer page with one of the background art designs that usually come with word-processing programs. Print your design on the side of the paper that does not include the box template.
- If you have a scanner, place leaves and flowers randomly on the scanner bed and scan. Save the scanned image as a document or photo file. Print the design on the plain side of the paper that does not include the box template.

3. Cut out the outer outline of the box.
4. Score the four curved inside fold lines by pressing with the tip of a wooden skewer, a metal fingernail file, or a tool made especially for paper crafting.
5. Fold the paper along the dotted center fold line with the decorative side facing outward. Crease by running your finger down the length of the fold.
6. Fold the small tab along the one edge toward the wrong side (undecorated side) and crease by running your finger down the length of the fold. Glue the tab to the wrong side of the other edge, forming the box sides.
7. Gently push in the scored, teardrop-shaped ends to close one end of the box. Slide soap in the box and close the other end.

An antique aluminum soap case will delight an antiques collector. (Aluminum does not react with fully cured soap.)

BOX PATTERN

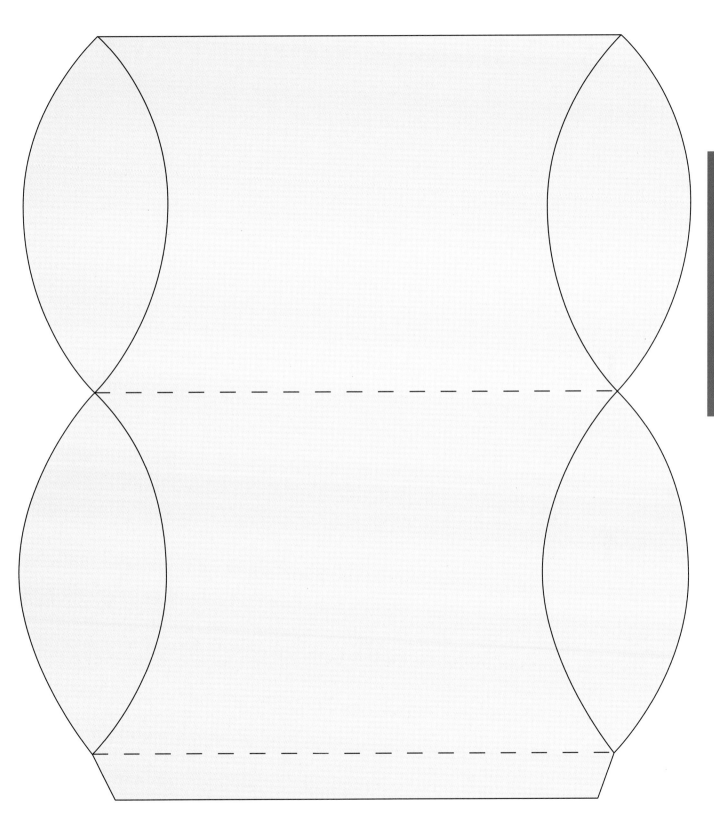

7

Handmade Equipment

Plastic and cardboard are fine to use for soap molds, and a board scraper/chopper does an adequate job of cutting soap logs into bars. If you view soap making as a potential lifelong craft, however, you may want to make a wood mold and bar cutter that will last for years and provide uniform results. The measurements given here can easily be enlarged to make molds and cutters that will accommodate larger batches of soap.

This sturdy wooden box mold can be made inexpensively with scrap wood, some fasteners, and common household tools, and it can be used for years. Although basic woodworking experience will make the job go faster, most crafters will be able to assemble this project easily by following the step-by-step instructions. If you don't want to cut your own wood to size, most lumber stores or chain hardware stores will cut the wood you buy from them to suit your needs.

Material and Tool List

Two pieces of 4¼-inch by 6¾-inch wood for the lid and bottom of the box (scraps of interior wall paneling are used here). A sturdy piece of cardboard could also be used for the lid, but not for the bottom.

Two pieces of 2½-inch by 3¾-inch wood (about ⅜ inch thick) for the short sides of the box (birch is used here)

Two pieces of 2½-inch by 6¾-inch wood (about ⅜-inch thick) for the long sides of the box

100-grit sandpaper

Eight 1-inch fasteners (round-head carpet nails are used here)

Ten 1-inch finish nails

Pencil

Drill and bit

Tack hammer

DRILL AND BIT
An electric, battery, or hand drill with a ¹⁄₁₆-inch bit is needed.

TACK HAMMER
A tack hammer works best for this small project, although a full-size hammer can be used, too.

1. Use the sandpaper to lightly sand the edges of all the wood pieces.

2. Then sand the top and bottom surfaces.

3. On one of the 2½-inch by 6¾-inch pieces, make a pencil mark about ³⁄₁₆ inch in from the top edge and right edge, as shown. Then make a mark ³⁄₁₆ inch in from the bottom edge and right edge.

4. Line up the edges of one long side and one short side. Note that the long edge is on top with the pencil marks visible. Hold both pieces together with one hand.

5. To drill a pilot hole through both pieces, place the drill bit on one of the marks. Make sure it's perpendicular (straight up and down) to the work surface.

6. Drill a hole through the long piece and into the short piece. The pilot hole should only be drilled ½ inch into the short piece.

7. With the long and short sides aligned, place a carpet nail into the pilot hole.

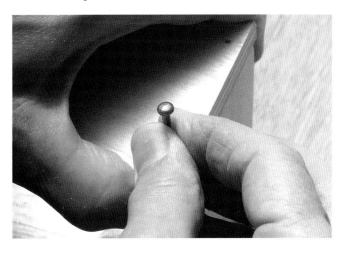

8. Use the tack hammer to drive a fastener into the pilot hole through the long and into the short side.

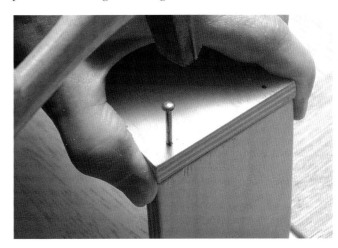

9. Place the drill bit on the second hole, making sure the drill is perpendicular to the work surface.

10. Drill the second pilot hole through the long side and ½ inch into the short side.

11. Drive the fastener into the pilot hole through the long and into the short side.

12. Repeat the process to attach the remaining long and short pieces to complete all four mold sides.

This is what the mold box should look like when all sides are attached.

13. Place the bottom piece of the mold on the mold sides, aligning all edges. Make ten evenly spaced pencil marks 3/16 inch from the edge at all four corners and along the short sides of the box.

14. Starting in one corner, hammer a finish nail through the top and the sides of the mold box.

15. Then hammer a finish nail between the two corners.

16. Continue fastening the top to the bottom at the pencil marks until all ten nails are in place.

Here is the box bottom after it has been attached to the sides of the mold box.

How to Make a Mold Liner

While it is not necessary to line a plastic soap mold, you must line a mold made of wood. Without a liner, the "hot" lye and oil mixture would eat away at the wood and cause it to splinter. Also, the finished soap would adhere to the wood surface, making it difficult to unmold the block.

Material and Tool List

Sheet of kitchen freezer paper cut to
    8½ inches by 11 inches
Binder clips
Pencil
Ruler
Clean work surface

BINDER CLIPS
Two-inch binder clips, available at office supply stores, are used to secure the mold liner to the mold.

KITCHEN FREEZER PAPER
Food freezer paper has a matte finish side and a waxy coated side, making it ideal to use as a durable, nonstick mold liner. It is readily available at most grocery stores.

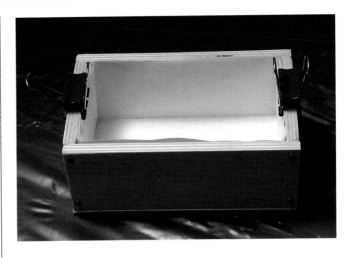

1. Place the freezer paper shiny-side-down on a clean work surface.

2. Near the top of the sheet on the long side, make a mark 2½ inches from the edge.

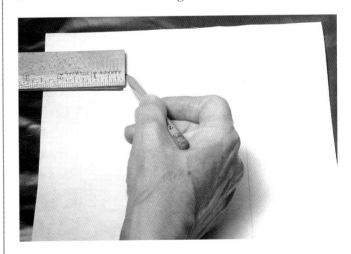

3. Do the same near the bottom of the page, making a mark 2½ inches from the edge.

4. Line up your ruler on the two lines and draw a line from the top edge to the bottom edge.

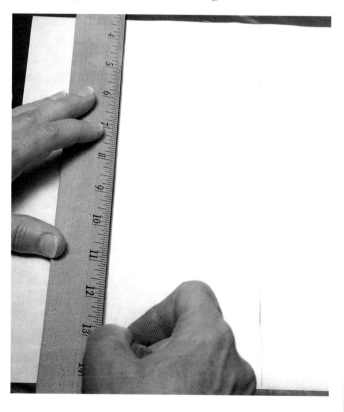

5. Turn the paper around so the unmarked side is on your left. Once again, mark 2½ inches from the edge at the top edge of the paper.

6. Then make a mark 2½ inches from the bottom.

7. As before, put the ruler on the marks and draw a line from the top to the bottom of the paper.

8. Repeat the process on both short sides by measuring in 2½ inches from the edge and drawing a line the entire length of the paper's short side. Finish marking the paper by repeating the process on the last short side.

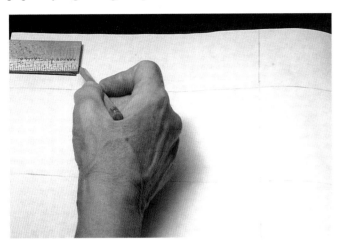

Your sheet of freezer paper should like this. The center rectangle should measure 3½ inches by 6 inches.

9. Next, flip the paper over so the shiny side is face up. Fold one of the shorts sides on the line so that the shiny sides are together.

10. Crease the fold with your finger.

11. Fold the other short sides together so that the shiny sides are together.

12. Crease that fold with your finger.

13. Repeat the process with one of the long sides. Fold the paper on the line so that it lies on top of the short side folds.

14. Fold the other long side toward the center so that it lies on top of the short sides and long sides.

15. Crease the fold.

16. Unfold one of the long edges of the paper. Grasp one of the corners and match the two short fold lines.

17. At one corner, match the short fold lines, forming a triangle.

18. Crease the fold.

19. Repeat the process of matching short fold lines and forming triangles on remaining sides. Crease the triangle folds as you go.

20. Fold the triangles in toward the center of the two short sides.

The short sides should look like this.

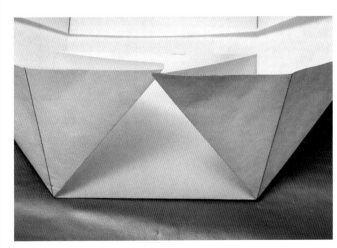

21. Gently place the liner in the mold box.

22. Secure with binder clips. If you don't have binder clips, masking tape can be used instead.

If you plan to make lots of cold process soap, you'll find this soap cutter to be a handy addition to your equipment list. It's easy to use and will ensure that each soap log is cut into even 1-inch bars.

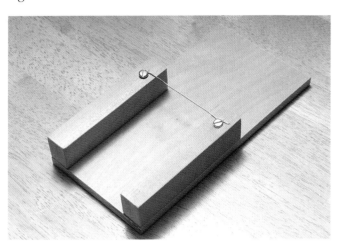

1. Line up the block with the left side edge and bottom edge.

Material and Tool List

One piece of 4-inch by 8-inch wood (³⁄₈ inch thick)
    (birch is shown in the photos)
Two pieces of 4¹⁄₂-inch by 1-inch by ³⁄₈-inch wood
    (pine is shown in the photos)
One 10-inch length of 20-gauge galvanized steel wire
Four 1-inch (#8) countersink screws
Two 1-inch (#6) screws
Drill with a #8 countersink drill bit
Screwdriver
Wire cutters
Tack hammer

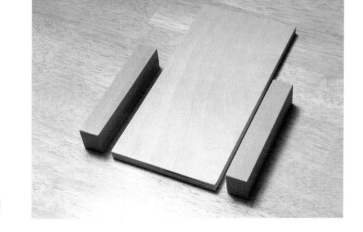

SCREWDRIVER
Use a screwdriver sized to fit your screws.

COUNTERSINK DRILL BIT
A countersink drill bit will enable you to drill a recessed hole so that the screw lies below the wood surface.

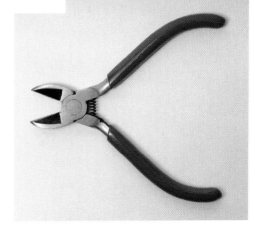

WOOD PIECES
Any type of scrap lumber may be used for this project.

WIRE CUTTERS
Any suitable wire-cutting tool can be used.

2. Trace the outline of the block onto the base.

3. Align the second block on the right edge and bottom edge as shown.

4. Trace the outline of this block on the base.

5. Make a pencil mark ⅜ inch from the edge and 4 inches from the bottom on the left side of the base.

6. Repeat by making a mark ⅜ inch from the edge and 4 inches from the right side of the base.

7. Now make pencil marks ⅜ inch from the edge and ½ inch from the bottom on the left and right sides of the base.

8. Place the two blocks under the base, aligning the bottom and outside edges of each block.

9. While holding the base and the blocks together firmly, drill a pilot hole at one of the marks, being careful to keep the drill perpendicular to the work surface.

10. Stop drilling when the countersink portion of the drill bit goes into the wood ⅛ inch.

11. Use a screwdriver and one of the four #8 countersink screws to join the base and the block.

12. Finish attaching the blocks to the base by drilling pilot holes on the other three marks and fastening the three remaining #8 screws.

13. Screw a #6 screw into the center of the block about ½ inch from the edge, as shown. Leave a small space between the wood and the screw to wrap the wire.

14. Leaving about a 2-inch tail on one end, wrap the wire around the screw one complete revolution.

15. Secure the wire by tightening the screw until it meets the wood surface.

16. Screw the second #6 screw into the center of the second block about ½ inch from the edges shown. Leave a small space between the wood and the screw to wrap the wire.

17. Grasp the long end of the wire and pull it across the base to the second screw.

18. Keeping the wire taut, wrap the wire completely around the screw.

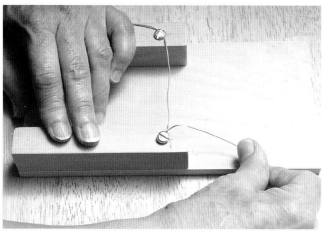

19. Pull the loose end of the wire to the outside.

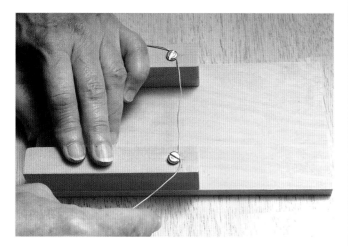

20. Secure the wire by tightening the screw until it meets the wood surface.

21. Cut the wire tail to about ¼ inch length.

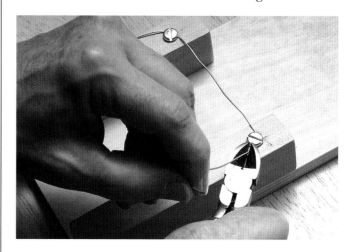

22. Using the tack hammer, pound the loose end into the wood.

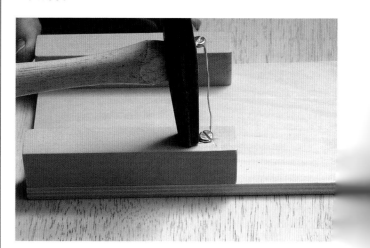

The wire is now securely fastened to the wood.

23. On the second side, cut the tail of wire to about ¼ inch.

24. Hammer that wire into the wood.

Your soap cutter is ready for use.

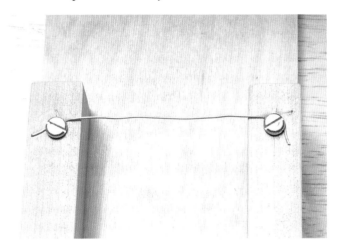

Resources

LYE
Hardware Stores: Lye is still sometimes sold as household drain cleaner under the name Rooto at small chain and family-owned hardware stores.

Camden-Grey Essential Oils, Inc.
3579 NW 82 Ave.
Doral, FL 33122
866-503-8615
www.essentialoil.net

SOAP-MAKING INGREDIENTS AND SUPPLIES
Emporium Naturals
One Pleasant St.
Cohasset, MA 02025
866-235-7914
www.emporiumnaturals.com

FromNatureWithLove.com
Natural Sourcing, LLC
341 Christian St.
Oxford, CT 06478
800-520-2060
www.fromnaturewithlove.com

Majestic Mountain Sage
918 West 700 North St., Suite 104
Logan, UT 84321
435-755-0863
www.thesage.com
(Website includes an online lye calculator)

Rainbow Meadow, Inc.
4494 Brooklyn Rd.
Jackson, MI 49201
800-207-4047
www.rainbowmeadow.com
(Website includes a soap recipe calculator)

Therapy Garden (online sales only)
www.therapygarden.com

BOTANICALS, COLORANTS, AND FRAGRANCE OILS
Atlantic Spice Company
2 Shore Road
North Truro, MA 02652
800-316-7965
www.atlanticspice.com

Bear Laboratories, Inc.
11820 Abilene Lane
Agua Dulce, CA 91350
661-268-0090
www.incenseoils.com
(Specializes in soap-grade fragrance oils.)

The Essential Oil Company
8225 SE 7th Ave.
Portland, OR 97202
800-729-5912
www.essentialoil.com

San Francisco Herb Company
250 14th St.
San Francisco, CA 94103
800-227-4530
www.sfherb.com

Symphony Scents
256 Broadway
Fort Edward, NY 12828
630-879-5404
www.symphonyscents.com

SOAP-MAKING GUILDS
The Handcrafted Soap Makers Guild, Inc.
P.O. Box 5103
Portland, OR 97208-5103
866-900-SOAP
www.soapguild.org
(An international, nonprofit professional trade association)